The KindEARTH Cookbook

ANASTASIA EDEN

Copyright © 2019 by Anastasia Eden

All rights reserved.

No part of this publication may be reproduced, stored in any retrieval system or transmitted in any form or by any means without prior permission from the publisher, except for brief quotations for review purposes.

Book design by Anastasia Eden

Photography by Anastasia Eden
except images on pages 12, 30, 54, 66, 86, 100, 126, 167 (Depositphotos)
and page 4 and back cover (Phyllis Lysionek)

ISBN 978-1-9161592-0-4

Visit: www.kindearth.net

For Cynthia & Jane
and the incredible light
that you have shone upon my path

"Be the change"

Welcome to the Kind Earth Cookbook!

I am here to take you on a journey of extraordinary culinary delight. It melts my heart to know that what I share might just bring a little bit more of the divine into this precious world. Everything here is wholesome and plant-based. This is not only beneficial for our precious planet and our fellow creatures, but it is also good for us. Eating in a healthy, compassionate way infuses our being with a plethora of nutrients, antioxidants and energy to help us experience optimal levels of health and wellness. It can change everything.

> *"Anastasia's meals are infused with a gentle love and deep respect for the ingredients, the finished product and for those for whom she is cooking. How can food ground the body and expand the soul with such sweet precision… be transportive in ways I couldn't imagine until experienced, and once experienced, I can't put into words? Somehow, Ana does it all with ease and grace."*
> Cynthia Nelson, Canada

I've enjoyed a completely plant-based life for 25 years. As a retreat chef, workshop leader and recipe developer, I feel deeply honoured to be able to show people how easy and joyful it is to prepare plant-based food.

This book is a celebration of life. People keep telling me how much they adore printed books, so I decided to take the best of my recipes from KindEarth.net to present a delightful medley of deliciousness in a book.

If we all make food from the heart, with compassionate, plant-based ingredients, just imagine the ripples that we will send out into the world. The taste, the sharing, the love, the joy! That's what the Kind Earth Cookbook is all about!

Let's get started and make
the world a better place,
one delectable bite at a time.

Anastasia x

Contents

WHY PLANT-BASED?
8 Kind for the planet
10 Kind for your health
11 Kind for our fellow animals

BREAKFAST
14 Plant-based milk 2 ways
16 Creamy coconut porridge
18 Pineapple bliss smoothie
20 Blueberry hempster smoothie
22 Green superfood smoothie
24 Maca mango smoothie
26 Chia mango pudding bowl
28 Almond maple granola
29 Raspberry breakfast compote

SALADS & DIPS
34 Cauliflower raw-slaw
   with walnut & raisin
35 Ginger beet raw-slaw
36 Lime pesto cauliflower
38 Bean & beetroot salad
   with black-eyed beans
39 Rainbow kale salad
   with mint infused dressing
40 Quinoa salad with turmeric
42 Beetroot hummus
43 Roast carrot & bean pâté
44 Raw sunflower seed pâté
46 Smoked paprika hummus
48 Hemp & lemon hummus
50 Parsley & lime guacamole
52 Creamy baba ganoush
   with a hint of smoked paprika

SOUPS
56 Turmeric & ginger soup
   with sweet potato & coconut milk
58 Creamy mushroom soup
60 Easy carrot coconut soup
   with ginger & paprika
61 Creamy tomato soup
   with sweet potato, rosemary & lentils
62 Chilli black bean soup
64 Creamy cauliflower soup

SIDES & OTHER THINGS
68 Milky matcha
69 Hot milky turmeric drink
   with cardamom & ginger
70 Mam's pickled Hawaiian daikon
72 Rosemary roast potatoes
73 Easy roasted brussel sprouts
74 Fresh mango chutney
76 Onion tamari gravy
78 Simple oatcake wraps
   with a cast iron skillet
80 Easy raspberry chia jam
81 Oven-baked flatbread
82 Scottish oatcakes
84 Soda loaf bread

BURGERS, SLICES & BITES

88 Spicy bean burgers
90 Beet Buddha bowl bites
92 Baked pakora
94 Sweet potato seed loaf
96 Sweet potato hemp burgers
98 Easy vegan burgers

MAIN MEALS

102 Black bean vegan tacos
103 Chickpea curry in 15 minutes
104 Lentil cottage pie
105 Easy ratatouille
106 Shepherd's pie, black bean style
108 Kind Earth curry
110 Butter bean coconut bake
112 Bolognese (kinda)
114 Spicy black bean one pot
116 Butternut & ginger noodle sauce
118 Golden veggie crumble pie
120 Sweet stuffed pepper
122 Winter squash one pot
124 Crustless vegan quiche

DESSERTS

128 Mango coconut ice cream
129 Blueberry nice cream
130 No churn cacao ice cream
132 Raw superfood brownies
134 Raw hemp seed brownies
136 Homemade vegan chocolate
138 Orange gingerbread cake
  chocolate style
140 La Palma island banana bread
142 Christmas sweet mince pies
144 Jam tarts
146 Raw strawberry cheesecake
148 Simple chocolate cupcakes
150 Sweet potato cacao cake
  with avocado chocolate frosting
152 Chocolate bodhi bars
154 Raw mango cheesecake
156 Vanilla shortbread cookies
158 Vegan chocolate cake
159 Blackberry & apple crumble

WHAT'S IN THE KIND EARTH PANTRY?

161 Seeds & nuts
162 Natural sweeteners & dried fruits
162 Spices & herbs
163 Helpful gluten-free flours
164 Superfoods
164 Condiments & helpful extras
165 Healthy fats & oils
166 Whole grains
167 Pulses

Why Plant-based?

"Never doubt that a small group of thoughtful, committed, citizens can change the world. Indeed, it is the only thing that ever has."
Margaret Mead

KIND FOR THE PLANET

Mother Earth breathes us into life. She holds us. She sustains us. She makes life possible and loves us so dearly. So what the heck has gone so wrong on this precious Earth? It seems that we are facing the sixth mass extinction with deforestation, over-fishing, pollution, loss of biodiversity, climate change and abuse of land and water use. It's happening on a mind-blowing scale. Nobody knows exactly what is going to happen from now on, but there is a plethora of research showing that eating a conscious, healthy plant-based diet is an important key to slowing down the damage so that we can regroup, take a deep inhale, and stand a chance of turning things around.

> Joseph Moore, a researcher at Oxford University says
> *"A vegan diet is probably the single biggest way to reduce your impact on planet Earth, not just greenhouse gases, but global acidification, eutrophication, land and water use".*

We need to open our hearts at this profound juncture in history and find a better way to co-exist with our precious Mother Earth. We have a choice, and an incredible power within us to choose a compassionate path forwards.

Researchers say that if we all went vegan and the land used previously for animals was allowed to revert to forest, the resulting carbon sequestration in vegetation stocks (carbon being captured and held in plants and soil) could be large enough to cancel out 300 years of all food-related greenhouse gas emissions (Bryngelsson et al,. 2016).

It may come as a surprise that livestock farming is responsible for more greenhouse gas emissions than all cars, buses, trains, plane and ships put together. This is due to actions such as deforestation, loss of carbon from grazing land, transportation of animal feed, energy used to grow feed and methane released from manure. Animal agriculture requires massive amounts of crops (to feed the animals that will be used as food) commandeering huge areas of land for single crops. This, in turn, destroys ecosystems on a large scale and strips the soil bare. Livestock farming wastes shocking amounts of water, whilst being responsible for freshwater pollution on a massive scale. It takes over 15,000 litres of water to produce 1kg of beef whilst it takes just over 300 litres of water to produce 1kg of vegetables. Mother Earth cannot counter-act the destruction and heal herself fast enough, so something must change. Thankfully we can start by making a huge difference, right now, simply by eating a plant-based diet.

> *Other things that can help to make the world a better place...*
>
> - **Support local organic farms when possible and try foraging.** *Local options vary. When I lived in the Canary Islands, eating locally meant that I was able to forage my own almonds and enjoy fresh lemons from the trees. Living in Britain I love to forage hazelnuts and walnuts in the autumn whilst making the most of raspberries, strawberries, blueberries and apples, which all grow in abundance. I try to make sure that at least 70% of my daily cuisine is from the country I am living in, favouring seasonal vegetables and fruits. Supporting local farms is also excellent for nurturing local communities, whilst cutting down on transportation and encouraging local ecosystem balance. Local, smaller organic farms tend to rotate crops and take better care of their immediate environment than larger industries.*
> - **Find fairly traded foods.** *The industrialised world has encouraged slave labour and inhumane working conditions. Look for fair-trade products and favour them where possible.*
> - **Compost your scraps.** *Return your peelings or food scraps back to Mother Earth to complete the cycle of life.*

KIND FOR YOUR HEALTH

I initially adopted a vegan diet because of compassion towards animals and Mother Earth, not particularly thinking about compassion for myself. This was 25 years ago, in the days before the internet, when I knew only two vegans who lived within a 50 mile radius. I had, however, seen a friend cure herself of leukaemia by eating a raw vegan diet and I'd seen my mother radically improve crippling arthritis by cutting out dairy. I couldn't help notice that I was also experiencing incredible levels of health, along with a sparkle and zest for life that I'd never known before. Fast forward more than a quarter of a century and it blows my mind to see all the evidence which confirms that eating a healthy plant-based diet is optimal for human health and reversing chronic disease.

The stories of people taking back their health by adopting a healthy vegan lifestyle are endless. Miraculous perhaps! I don't really believe that these are miracles; I suspect that it is simply how it's supposed to be. The body has an innate capacity to heal itself once we get our minds out of the way and begin to create optimal conditions for health.

It is thought that one of the reasons plant-based diets are so effective for supporting health is because plant foods do not contain dietary cholesterol. Add an abundance of antioxidants, anti-inflammatories, fibre, heart-healthy fats and supportive nutrients and we are talking about something quite profoundly healing. On the other hand, animal products such as meat, eggs and dairy contain large amounts of cholesterol and saturated fats, which can lead to clogging the arteries with plaque and significantly increase the risk of conditions such as heart disease.

I must add that not all vegan diets are healthy. You can still get vegan junk food. A balanced diet varies for everyone, but with plant-based, it will typically include healthy fats (nuts, seeds, avocado, olives etc.), vegetables, dark leafy greens, fruits, some grains (i.e. rice, quinoa, oats), legumes and pulses (i.e. beans, lentils, peas).

Don't worry too much about whether you are getting enough protein. The protein thing is a bit of a myth. A balanced plant-based diet means that you'll get more than enough protein for optimal human health. If you eat a good mix of plant-foods you will easily get all the amino acids you need to create a healthy abundance of protein in your body (protein deficiency only tends to be an issue if people eat a calorie restricted diet over an extended period of time or don't get enough variety).

The most comprehensive study on the implications of a plant-based diet for health was the 'China Study', a study conducted over 40+ years by Cornell University, Oxford University, the Chinese Academy of Preventive Medicine and Dr. Campbell's 40 years of biomedical research. With 650,000 workers and the best medical researchers available they collected data from 880 million Chinese citizens. After this extensive body of research, Dr Campbell strongly advocates eating a whole food, plant-based diet. He concludes that a diet with low (or no) animal protein will greatly reduce your risk of cancer, heart disease, auto-immune disease, osteoporosis, diabetes and many other serious diseases.

The China Study examines the link between the consumption of animal products (including dairy) and chronic illnesses such as coronary heart disease, diabetes, breast cancer, prostate cancer, and bowel cancer. The authors concluded that people who eat a predominantly whole-food, plant-based diet, avoiding animal products and reducing their intake of processed foods and refined carbohydrate will escape, reduce, or reverse the development of numerous diseases.

KIND FOR OUR FELLOW ANIMALS

Compassion towards animals is the clearest of all reasons to adopt a plant-based diet. Nobody wants other beings to suffer. Yet it seems that deep within the subconscious of today's society there is a sort of mass cognitive dissonance, a mass empathy-amnesia towards sentient life, where inhumanity to other beings has been normalised. I think perhaps it plays on our deep primordial fear of being cast out of the tribe, hence going along with whatever culture decides is normal, along with its empty promises of safety and a good life. Empathy has been abandoned in selective areas of life as we've convinced ourselves that we need to eat animals to survive and that they taste good.

No animal wants to be in captivity. No animal wants to suffer. Animals feel pain just like we do. Animals grieve and feel emotions in similar ways to humans. No mother wants to have her child taken from her at birth. Cow's milk was designed by nature for calves, not humans and 75% of the population of the planet is lactose intolerant for a good reason.

When animals such as chickens and cows (that are normally eaten as food) live in environments where they are free to be themselves, they exhibit affectionate, natural behaviour and show love for fellow animals and humans.

I invite us all to look deep within, to open our hearts and treat all sentient beings with the same respect and love that we wish to experience ourselves.

Breakfast & Mornings

How to make plant-based milk 2 ways

You might be surprised how easy it is to make your own plant-based milk. I favour nuts that are available more locally. For me in Britain that would be walnuts and hazelnuts, and when I lived in the Canary Islands I was surrounded by almond trees. I buy local hemp seeds when possible too. You will need a nut milk bag for harder nuts like walnuts (as described in the first recipe). If you use hemp seeds (or cashew nuts) then straining is optional. Have fun!

Walnut Milk

Ingredients

100g walnuts
750ml (approx) pure water
Dash of vanilla (optional)
3 pitted dates (optional but nice)

How to make

1. Soak the walnuts overnight (or for a few hours) to soften them. You can also blend without soaking if you forget or don't have time to soak ahead (the nuts are just a little harder that's all).
2. Drain and then rinse with water.
3. Put into a blending jug, add about 750ml of water and then blend for around one minute. This works in a cheap blender or a high powered blender.
4. Strain the blended milk through a nut bag and squeeze.
5. Pour into a glass bottle, jug or jar. Pop on the lid and then chill it in the fridge. Shake before using.

Hemp Seed Milk

Ingredients

100g shelled hemp seeds
500ml pure water
1 teaspoon vanilla extract
2 teaspoons coconut sugar

How to make

1. Add all ingredients to a jug for blending.
2. Blend for about a minute or until everything is combined.
3. Pop the hemp milk into a large jar or bottle.
4. Put it into the fridge to chill before serving (it tastes best chilled).
5. You will still get some sediment settling from the hemp seeds. This is all super healthy.
6. Note: If you don't want the sediment OR if you have used whole hemp seeds (i.e. seeds that aren't shelled) then you will need to strain it with a cheese cloth or purpose made nut milk bag.
7. Give it a swish and a jiggle before using.

Creamy Coconut Porridge
WITH CINNAMON

A gorgeous, rolled oat porridge with creamed coconut, cinnamon and coconut sugar.

Serves: 1   Time: 15 minutes

Ingredients

75g rolled oats
500ml water (approx)
25g creamed coconut
1 heaped tablespoon coconut sugar
1 heaped teaspoon ground cinnamon

How to make

1. Measure your oats, pop them in the pan with the water. Turn on the heat to a medium level. Add about half the water to start with (add the rest as required during the cooking period).
2. Add the coconut sugar and stir the porridge regularly so that it doesn't stick to the bottom of the pan.
3. Slice or grate the creamed coconut. This will quickly melt upon heating.
4. Halfway through cooking add the creamed coconut and cinnamon.
5. Mix in thoroughly.
6. Continue to stir and add water as required. The oats will readily absorb the liquid.
7. Your porridge will be ready to eat after 10 to 15 minutes. I like to give it 15 minutes just to make sure the oats are thoroughly cooked.
8. You can also cook for 10 minutes, turn off the heat and come back 15 minutes later to enjoy (handy if you are getting ready for work or want to pop into the shower).
9. If you prefer it sweeter then add more coconut sugar. Likewise, if you want more coconut or cinnamon, just play with the ingredients to get your perfect porridge.

Pineapple Bliss Smoothie

A blissful pineapple smoothie experience with bananas and almond butter. This can be used for a smoothie bowl or sipped from a glass.

Serves: 1 to 2   Time: 5 minutes

Ingredients

- 2 bananas (medium sized)
- 2 handfuls frozen pineapple
- 1 tablespoon almond butter
- 100ml plant-based milk (or water)

How to make

1. Peel two ripe bananas (ripe is best for sweetness).
2. Put in a jug.
3. Add two handfuls of frozen pineapple.
4. Add one tablespoon of almond butter.
5. Add 100ml of plant-based milk. You can use any plant milk or even water for this.
6. Blend until creamy smooth.
7. Enjoy in a glass or as a smoothie bowl (with favourite toppings).

Let's talk about pineapples

Did you know, if you twist the top off a pineapple and plant it in the soil, then a couple of years later you will have a new pineapple grow out of that? I just love the miracle of nature.

The best known benefit of pineapples is from the bromelain enzyme (I believe that pineapple may be the only source of this enzyme). Bromelain is said to break down complex proteins, which helps aid digestion. This rather clever enzyme is also supposed to have top-notch anti-inflammatory benefits and has been shown to help improve symptoms of arthritis.

Blueberry Hempster Smoothie
WITH HOMEMADE PLANT-BASED MILK

A superfood smoothie with shelled hemp seeds to infuse your body with goodness.

Serves: 1 glass   Time: 5 minutes

Ingredients

1 large ripe banana
100g frozen blueberries
2 tablespoons shelled hemp seeds
250ml homemade plant-based milk

How to make

1. Peel and slice banana.
2. Blend all ingredients together until creamy smooth. You can use a hand blender for this or a regular jug blender.
3. If you don't have a batch of homemade homemade milk ready (see page 14 for walnut or hemp milk) then use any other plant-based milk or even water.
4. Enjoy immediately to your heart's delight.

Tips for a deliciously sweet smoothie every time

One of the important keys to getting your smoothie deliciously sweet is in the banana. Be sure that your banana is ripe (no green bits on the outer skin and preferably starting to get brown spots). Green bananas are a rich source of carbohydrates, although they are starchy and at this stage their natural sweetness has not yet developed. As soon as it starts to ripen, the carbohydrate levels rapidly decrease and turn into desirable fruit sugars, delivering that creamy, yummy sweetness that most of us adore.

Green Superfood Smoothie

A green kale smoothie with pineapple, avocado, hemp seeds and dates. An excellent way to pack a massive amount of nutrients into a glass.

Makes: 3 glasses   Time: 5 minutes

Ingredients

250ml to 500ml water
1 large handful of kale leaves
1 medium to large pineapple
1 medium avocado
8 pitted dates
4 tablespoons shelled hemp seeds

How to make

1. You can use frozen or fresh pineapple. If using frozen, let it defrost a little to make it easier to blend.
2. Slice the avocado in half, take out the seed and then scoop out the flesh.
3. If your blender isn't strong then chop your kale leaves finely to help them process. Alternatively, if your blender is strong then you can put the leaves in whole.
4. Blend 250ml of water with the kale first, until the greens are broken down.
5. Add all other ingredients to the blender. If you have a high powered blender you can get away with using less water. If your blender isn't very strong then it might help to add more water. It will be easier to blend if your pineapple is not frozen.
6. Blend the ingredients until blended smoothly. If the ingredients refuse to blend to start with because the ingredients are too thick, then use a spatula to scrape down the sides and blend again (repeat several times if necessary).
7. Serve immediately in a glass or as a smoothie bowl.

Maca Mango Smoothie
FOR NATURAL HORMONE BALANCE

A ridiculously healthy maca and mango smoothie to help balance the hormones naturally.

Makes: 1 glass   Time: 5 minutes

Ingredients

200g frozen mango
1 ripe banana
1 heaped teaspoon maca powder
1 teaspoon ground flaxseed
1 tablespoon tahini
150ml plant-based milk (or water)
1 teaspoon ginger (optional)

How to make

1. You can use fresh mango for this rather than frozen, although if you do use fresh, you might want to leave out a little of the liquid (frozen keeps the smoothie thick).
2. Finely grate the ginger if you are opting to use it.
3. Put all of the ingredients into a blender.
4. Stop and scrape down the sides if necessary.
5. Blend until creamy smooth.
6. Enjoy immediately.

What is maca all about?

Natives from the mountains of Peru, have used this plant to counteract hormonal issues for centuries. Not only does it help with the obvious hormonal things, it supports with stressful situations, where 'fight or flight' mode has a tendency to go into total overdrive.

Maca is good for all-around hormone support for everyone. Sexual and reproductive health and libido are usually the first things that spring to mind when we think of hormones, all of which are greatly supported by maca. However, they are just the tip of the iceberg. Hormones are in fact chemical messengers that tell our cells what they need to do, regulating the balance of our entire body. Hormone function includes digestion control, sleep regulation, brain development, mood, heart behaviour, blood pressure, fat metabolism, skin health, mental health, immune system, reproductive health, sexual health and bone maintenance. Hormones also manage our 'fight or flight' response, induce calm, and control the rate at which we age. Maca's powerful ability to balance hormones make it one incredible plant food to include in your daily life.

Chia Mango Pudding Bowl
For Breakfast

A super healthy plant-based chia breakfast pudding bowl recipe, using mangoes, banana, tahini.

Serves: 2 to 4   Time: 5 minutes (plus soaking)

Ingredients

1 ripe mango (medium sized)
200ml to 250ml water (or plant milk)
1 ripe banana (optional)
2 heaped teaspoons of tahini (or cashew butter)
3 tablespoons chia seeds
Optional superfoods

How to make

1. Peel and scoop out the mango and place into a blending jug.
2. Add the water (or plant-milk), banana, tahini and any optional superfoods.
3. Blend until smooth.
4. Mix in the chia seeds.
5. Over the next 20 minutes, stir again a couple of times. Re-stirring in this period stops the seeds sticking together.
6. Pop in the fridge overnight (or for at least an hour or two).
7. Serve the next morning (or a couple of hours after making).
8. Add toppings of your choice such as fresh fruit, dried fruit, nuts, seeds, granola etc.

If you've not yet discovered the culinary alchemy of chia seeds, then you are in for a real treat. When soaked, they thicken, in a jelly-like fashion, making the perfect pudding or smoothie addition. Soaking also makes it easier to digest and assimilate their nutrients. Chia seeds are one of the richest plant-based sources of essential fats. They are also a high quality, complete protein food and loaded with antioxidants.

Almond & Maple Granola

A delicious granola recipe made with oats, almonds and sweetened with maple syrup. Baked in the oven and enjoyed for breakfast.

Time: 50 minutes

Ingredients

- 100g almonds (blanched or regular)
- 750g rolled oats
- 50g pumpkin seeds
- 2 heaped tablespoons ground cinnamon
- 150ml maple syrup
- 100ml coconut oil
- 2 teaspoons almond extract
- 50g to 100g raisins

How to make

1. Break up the almonds a little bit if you want to, with a pestle and mortar. Alternatively just leave them whole, it's up to you.
2. Put all the dry ingredients into a large oven-proof dish, and give them a quick mix.
3. Add the maple syrup, coconut oil, and almond extract and mix thoroughly until everything is evenly combined. You can do this with a spoon or your hands (or both).
4. Compact down gently into the baking dish.
5. Pop into a pre-heated oven at gas mark 6 (200°C/400°F) for about 45 minutes.
6. During the baking period mix the ingredients several times with a spoon.
7. When baked, take out and allow to cool down.
8. Add a large handful of raisins.
9. Enjoy!

Raspberry Breakfast Compote
with apple & vanilla

A warming stewed fruit compote with vanilla, a hint of coconut sugar and ginger.

Serves: 1 to 2   Time: 15 minutes

Ingredients

3 organic apples (medium sized)
2 tablespoons water
Handful of raspberries
1 teaspoon vanilla extract
1 heaped teaspoon coconut sugar
Pinch of ground ginger (optional)

How to make

1. Chop the apples into tiny cubes. There is no need to peel them as there are lots of nutrients to be found in, and just beneath, the skin. That said, if you are opting for cooking apples (which tend to have a thicker, waxier skin) rather than normal sweet apples, then do peel them. If you are using non-organic apples, then definitely peel.
2. Pop your cubed apple pieces into a pan along with 2 tablespoons of water. Turn on the stove and heat up. Stir regularly and replace the lid between stirrings to help the cooking process. Be sure not to add too much water, as a couple of tablespoons should be more than enough to get the cooking process started. Allow to cook gently for about 10 to 15 minutes.
3. Add in the raspberries, coconut sugar, vanilla and optional pinch of ginger and cook for a further couple of minutes.
4. Use the back of a spoon to help break down the cooked apples.
5. Enjoy right away with a sprinkle of granola, muesli or dairy-free yoghurt.

Salads & Dips

And so it is... salad doesn't have to be boring ever!
"Vancouver Island Workshop, making Buddha Bowls"

Cauliflower Salad 3 Delicious Ways

Cauliflower makes an excellent addition to a salad. The next three recipes are all inspired by this delightful, versatile vegetable. I am sharing these to show you how one simple ingredient can transform salad into a divine plate of alchemy.

1. Cauliflower Raw-slaw
with walnut & raisin

Lovingly throw in some walnuts and raisins, mix in the delectable creamy tahini sauce and yes please!

Serves: 4   Time: 5 minutes

Ingredients

1 small cauliflower
Handful of raisins
Handful of walnuts

Tahini Sauce
5 tablespoons tahini
1 teaspoon maple syrup
1 tablespoon tamari (or shoyu)
1 tablespoon apple cider vinegar
4 tablespoons water (or as required)
Twist of black pepper (optional)

How to make

1. Chop the cauliflower into small pieces (which will look nice if you retain some of the 'florets').
2. Keep some of the leaves, if you have nice ones, and finely chop them.
3. Make the sauce by first mixing the tahini, maple syrup, tamari and apple cider vinegar with a spoon. Tahini can sometimes go 'claggy' when you first mix it. If this happens, keep mixing, it will eventually become smooth as you gradually add in the water during the next step.
4. Add the water a little at a time and mix in. The amount of water will depend on the thickness of your tahini. You are looking for a lovely thick pouring consistency.
5. Add a twist of black pepper (optional).
6. Mix the sauce into the cauliflower.
7. Add the walnuts and raisins.
8. Serve along with other salads as part of a buffet or with cooked quinoa or rice. This also works well with a dip and crackers.

2. Ginger Beet Raw-slaw
with cauliflower

A super healthy ginger raw-slaw with beetroot, cauliflower and a vegan tahini sauce.

Serves: 3   Time: 10 minutes

Ingredients

Sauce

2 tablespoons tahini
1 tablespoon raw apple cider vinegar
1 tablespoon tamari (or shoyu)
1 to 2 tablespoons water
1 teaspoon fresh ginger (finely grated)
1 teaspoon maple syrup
1 teaspoon ground coriander

Veggies & things

1 small cauliflower
1 beetroot (tennis ball size)
1 small onion (golf ball sized)
Handful of raisins (or sultanas)

How to make

1. Make the tahini sauce by putting all the sauce ingredients into a small blending jug and blending with a hand blender. Alternatively mix the sauce by hand in a small jug. If you do mix by hand then don't add all the water at once - but rather add it in stages. The tahini often forms stubborn lumps or clags together unless you add liquid gradually. Mix until creamy smooth.
2. Chop the cauliflower into tiny florets or tiny pieces. Also chop the leaves, if there are any good ones.
3. Grate the beetroot (removing any tough end bits first).
4. Finely chop the onion.
5. Put the chopped cauliflower, grated beetroot, chopped onion and raisins in a salad bowl.
6. Mix in the sauce until everything is nicely coated.
7. Enjoy as part of a salad buffet, with potato wedges or a quinoa dish.

3. Lime Pesto Cauliflower

A super healthy vegan salad with cauliflower and a cashew, lime, and basil pesto dressing. Filling, nutritious and a real crowd pleaser.

Serves: 2 to 4   Time: 10 minutes (plus soaking)

Ingredients

Pesto ingredients

100g cashews
35g basil (one large handful)
Zest of one lime
Juice of 2 limes
(or 4 tablespoons lime juice)
1 garlic clove (small)
½ teaspoon sea salt
1 teaspoon rice syrup (or maple syrup)

Salad ingredients

1 small cauliflower
1 small apple

How to make

1. Soak the cashews in water overnight or for at least three hours.
2. After soaking, drain the cashews and put into a jug ready for blending.
3. Finely grate the zest from one lime into the drained cashews.
4. Juice the limes.
5. Crush the garlic and remove the skin.
6. Add the lime juice, garlic, basil, sea salt and rice syrup into the blending jug.
7. Blend until it turns as creamy as you can get it. I find this easiest with a high powered hand blender, to really 'get in there' and blend it up nicely.
8. Chop the cauliflower into small florets (or alternatively chop into large chunks and toss into the food processor to create a 'cauliflower rice').
9. Chop the apple into very small cubes.
10. Mix the pesto with the apple and cauliflower until everything is evenly coated.

36   The KindEARTH Cookbook

Bean & Beetroot Salad
with black-eyed beans & tahini sauce

A hearty black-eyed bean, beetroot, broccoli and raisin salad with a creamy sauce to dress and flavour.

Serves: 3   Time: 5 minutes

Ingredients

Tahini sauce ingredients
2 heaped tablespoons tahini
1 teaspoon rice syrup (or maple syrup)
½ teaspoon sea salt
Twist of pepper
1 tablespoon apple cider vinegar
2 teaspoons water (or more if needed)

Salad ingredients
1 beetroot (tennis ball sized)
1 very small broccoli
125g (½ can) black eyed-beans (drained)
Small handful raisins

How to make

1. Make the sauce by mixing all sauce ingredients together in a bowl. Tahini can be a little stubborn at times - if this is the case, then just keep mixing until it creams up. Tahini can also come in different consistencies, depending on the brand. If yours is really thick, then simply add a little more water. If it is super-thin, then you might leave the water out all together.
2. Make sure the beetroot is clean and remove the top & tail with a sharp knife. Grate the beetroot (with skin still on) into your salad bowl.
3. Finely chop the broccoli and add to the bowl.
4. Toss the drained black-eyed beans and raisins in with the salad.
5. Mix in the tahini dressing well.
6. Eat on its own as a hearty salad or a part of a salad buffet. This works really well on top of rice, quinoa or millet too.

Rainbow Kale Salad
with mint infused dressing

A delicious recipe for super healthy kale rainbow salad with a fresh mint infused dressing.

Serves: 3 to 4   Time: 10 minutes

Ingredients

Dressing ingredients:
Handful of fresh garden mint
3 tablespoons of rice vinegar
2 tablespoons flax oil
3 tablespoons olive oil
½ to 1 teaspoon maple syrup (optional)
½ medium sized apple

Salad ingredients:
5 large kale leaves
5 large romaine lettuce leaves
½ an apple
½ small yellow sweet pepper
½ small red sweet pepper
4 large celery stalks
1 medium ripe avocado

How to make

1. Make the dressing first by de-stalking the mint and then blending all of the dressing ingredients together in a blender.
2. Chop the salad ingredients as desired or as follows…
3. Chop the kale and romaine lettuce into thin bite-sized pieces.
4. Chop the apple into very small cubes, with the skin still intact.
5. De-stem and de-seed the sweet pepper, then slice or cube.
6. Slice celery into small pieces.
7. Score squares into the avocado and scoop out.
8. Mix everything together with the salad dressing until it is all evenly coated.

The KindEARTH Cookbook

Quinoa Salad
with turmeric & warming spices

This medley works well as part of a salad, in a wrap, as part of a Buddha bowl, or with a Mexican feast.

Serves: 4   Time: 30 minutes

Ingredients

- 100g quinoa
- 1 teaspoon coconut oil
- 350ml water
- ¼ teaspoon black pepper
- ½ teaspoon ground turmeric
- 1 teaspoon ground coriander
- ½ teaspoon smoked paprika
- Small handful fresh parsley
- 2 spring onions
- ½ red sweet pepper
- 1 teaspoon toasted sesame oil
- 1 tablespoon hemp oil
- 1 tablespoon tamari

How to make

1. Gently toast the quinoa. Toast in a medium sized pan by first heating a teaspoon of coconut or olive oil. Toss in the quinoa and then stir occasionally over two or three minutes. You will start to get a slightly toasted aroma when it is ready (be sure not to over-toast it).
2. Add the water to the quinoa.
3. Add the turmeric and black pepper and put the lid on the pan.
4. Bring the contents to the boil and then allow to simmer. It should take about 20 minutes to fully cook the quinoa, at which point all of the water should be absorbed. Mix in the ground coriander and paprika at this stage.
5. Allow the quinoa to cool.
6. Finely chop the parsley and spring onions.
7. Chop the red pepper into small squares.
8. When the quinoa has cooled to room temperature add all remaining ingredients and mix in.
9. Serve immediately if desired. This also keeps fine for up to three days in the fridge.

Quinoa is an ancient seed that thinks it is a grain

Quinoa (pronounced keen-wah) is thought to have originated with Incan cultures thousands of years ago in the regions around Peru, Chile and Bolivia. It comes in all sorts of different colours and there are now strains that grow successfully in temperate climates like Britain, giving this ancient crop much more potential as a sustainable crop. It is actually a seed (although we love to use it in place of a grain). If you grow your own then the leaves can be eaten just like spinach.

Beetroot Hummus

A magical dance of flavour. Delicious, nutritious and hands up who loves that colour!

Serves: 8   Time: 50 minutes

Ingredients

- 200g (approx) beetroot
- Juice of 1½ lemons
- 2 cloves of garlic
- 200g chickpeas (cooked)
- 1 teaspoon sea salt
- 7 tablespoons tahini
- 3 tablespoons water
- 1 tablespoon tamari

How to make

1. Clean the beetroot and then cut the rough end off and discard.
2. Cube the beetroot (1½cm or ½ an inch works well) or slice it and bake in the oven for about 45 minutes.
3. Juice the lemons.
4. Crush the garlic.
5. Blend all ingredients together in a food processor or blender until smooth.
6. Allow to chill before serving.

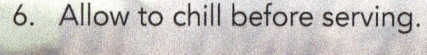

Roast Carrot & Bean Pâté

A delectable, flavoursome, nutrient-rich pâté made with roast carrots, black beans and a medley of warming spices. A potluck or party size portion.

Serves: 12   Time: 60 minutes

Ingredients

400g cooked black turtle beans
750g carrots
1 clove of garlic
Juice of 1 medium lemon
Pinch of lemon rind
1 teaspoon ginger (finely grated)
2 teaspoons ground coriander
1 teaspoon garam masala
2 teaspoons sea salt

How to make

1. If you aren't using pre-cooked beans, you will need to soak and cook them ahead of time. Drain when done and allow to cool for a little while.
2. Leave the skins on the carrots (unless they are not organic), and slice into finger-sized pieces. Dry roast in an oven until you can pierce a fork through them. This might take about 30 - 45 minutes on a high temperature. (Note: if you are baking something else at the same time, then simply bake on whatever temperature is happening). Allow to cool for a little while once baked.
3. Crush the garlic and remove the skin.
4. Juice the lemon.
5. Finely grate a big pinch of lemon rind.
6. Peel and finely grate the ginger.
7. Blend all ingredients together to create a good pâté consistency. I would use either a powerful hand-blender or a high powered jug blender.
8. Chill before serving.
9. This serves really well with homemade oatcakes and a tasty salad.

Raw Sunflower Seed Pâté
and the divine spark of the cosmos

A vibrant pâté using soaked and sprouted sunflower seeds with coriander, raw garlic and lemon.

Serves: 6   Time: 5 minutes (plus soaking)

Ingredients

- 100g raw sunflower seeds
- Juice of 2 lemons
- Lemon zest (up to 1 teaspoon)
- 1 clove of garlic
- 1 bunch (60g) coriander leaves
- 1 teaspoon sea salt
- 1 heaped teaspoon ground coriander

How to make

1. Soak the sunflower seeds overnight (or for at least 7 hours), then drain and rinse.
2. Juice the lemons and add to jug with soaked seeds.
3. Finely grate up to 1 teaspoon of lemon zest (to your preferred zingi-ness).
4. Crush garlic.
5. Roughly chop coriander leaves.
6. Add all ingredients to the jug and blend until everything is blended together beautifully.

Melting into the cosmos

This is no ordinary recipe, it is the ultimate vibration raising pâté! We soak the sunflower seeds overnight, which starts the spouting process. Soaking unleashes an incredible life force from a dormant, raw seed. It's the same miraculous life force that wants to turn a tiny, humble seed into a glorious vibrant sunshine-yellow flower!

Seeds are essentially sleeping until they become activated. Soaking them in water wakes them up. So you aren't just eating sunflower seeds anymore - you are eating a divine spark of the cosmos!

Smoked Paprika Hummus

Hummus fulfils that need for something creamy, tasty and satiating. This one is a delectable citrus, tahini, garlic, chickpea, smoked paprika fusion. Best ever!

Serves: 6   Time: 5 minutes

Ingredients

3 tablespoons lemon juice
200g chickpeas (cooked)
3 tablespoons tahini
½ teaspoon sea salt
1 teaspoon smoked paprika
1 large clove of garlic
4 tablespoons water

How to make

1. Blend all the ingredients together using either a food processor, jug blender or hand blender until creamy smooth.
2. You can eat this right away, although it works best when chilled first.
3. Serves well with pita bread, crackers or with salad.
4. Don't forget to add a sprinkle of paprika on top to be posh.

A note about tahini

Tahini is a beautiful creamy paste made from sesame seeds. It is an essential ingredient for hummus making. There are lots of different brands of tahini out there, all with different tastes (and to be quite honest, it can be a bit off-putting if you get a grainy bitter one). If you can, make sure you get a creamy, delicious version of tahini. I must warn you though, if you stumble on to a delicious source, you'll probably get hooked on the stuff, just like I have!

Hemp & Lemon Hummus

A delicious and super-nutritious hemp hummus, using shelled hemp seed hearts. Made with a big heart full of love.

Serves: 8   Time: 5 minutes

Ingredients

- 2 large cloves garlic
- Juice of 2 lemons
- ¼ teaspoon organic lemon rind
- 250g cooked chickpeas
- 75g hulled hemp seeds
- 6 tablespoons tahini
- 2 tablespoons hemp oil
- 4 tablespoons water
- 1 teaspoon salt
- 1 teaspoon ground coriander

How to make

1. Crush the garlic.
2. Juice the lemon (make sure it is organic, unwaxed and give it a wash first).
3. Finely grate lemon rind.
4. Blend all ingredients together until creamy smooth with either a hand-blender, jug blender or food processor.

Why are hemp seeds so good for us?

It has to be said, hemp is one of the most amazing plant foods that exists on our planet. It is a protein-power-superstar, having one of the most complete protein profiles in the plant food kingdom. It contains a fabulous balance of essential fats (essential fats are crucial to include in your diet for health) including omega 3. It is excellent for skin health, cholesterol levels and is especially high in beneficial antioxidants.

Which hemp seeds should we use?

Hemp seeds are available in all good health food stores (in most countries). I am not talking about the hemp with the high THC levels that gets you high; I am talking about the culinary hemp seeds. It is important to buy shelled hemp seeds (also called hemp hearts or hulled hemp seeds) without the crunchy outer shell on them, because it makes it very easy to blend them into your cuisine.

Parsley & Lime Guacamole

A delicious artisan, parsley and lime guacamole recipe using finely chopped onions for a flavourful avocado based dip.

Serves: 3   Time: 5 minutes

Ingredients

1 large avocado
Juice of 1 lime
Handful of fresh parsley
2 tablespoons chopped onion
Sea salt (to taste)
Pepper (to taste)

How to make

1. Make sure the avocado is ripe.
2. Scoop it into a bowl and mash with a fork.
3. Juice the lime and add to the bowl.
4. Chop the parsley and add to the bowl.
5. Finely chop about 2 tablespoons worth of onion and add to the bowl.
6. Add salt and pepper to taste then mash everything together with a fork until evenly combined.
7. Enjoy the same day.

Tips on choosing a good avocado

- A ripe or semi-ripe avocado is essential for a divine avocado experience.
- Your avocado should feel heavy-ish in weight.
- Avoid ones that look bruised with signs of decay or loose skin.
- Minor blemishes or scuffs that come from being on the tree are natural and fine.
- You know it is ripe when it yields softly to gentle pressure on its skin.
- If it is not ripe then it will feel solid and won't 'give' to your fingers when you press it gently but if you are buying from a reliable source then it should ripen within a few days at room temperature.
- You can usually buy them in the store either ripe or unripe (sometimes you don't get the choice).

Creamy Baba Ganoush
with a hint of smoked paprika

A smoky aubergine dip from the Middle East, using a pinch of smoked paprika for a gentle smoked flavour.

Serves: 4   Time: 45 minutes

Ingredients

1 large aubergine/eggplant (about ½ kg in weight)
1 small garlic clove
1 tablespoon (approx) lemon juice
2 tablespoons tahini
½ teaspoon sea salt
¼ teaspoon smoked ground paprika
Twist of black pepper

Optional garnish

Drizzle hemp oil
Few parsley sprigs
Sprinkle ground paprika

How to make

1. Score through the aubergine (also called eggplant) several times with a sharp knife. This is important to stop it bursting open in the oven when you bake it.
2. Bake it in a hot oven at gas mark 7 (220°C/425°F) between 40 and 60 minutes (or until soft).
3. Once baked, allow to cool.
4. When cool, scoop out the contents. If your aubergine is quite watery (as most of them are) then it's best to drain off quite a bit of the excess water. If there is too much water, then you won't get it to cream up as well as you might like. Use a colander or sieve and let it drain for a minute or two.
5. When ready, put the strained aubergine into a jug or food processor.
6. Crush the garlic and add to the jug.
7. Add the lemon juice, tahini, sea salt, smoked paprika and pepper.
8. Blend until creamy smooth (I normally do this with a hand blender, but a food processor or jug blender will well work too).
9. Chill before serving.
10. You can add optional garnish of parsley, smoked paprika or hemp oil, if you like when serving.

Soups

Turmeric & Ginger Soup
with sweet potato & coconut milk

This sunshine coloured soup is filled with nutritional benefits and a playful dance of warming spices.

Serves: 3   Time: 20 minutes

Ingredients

2 large sweet potatoes (700g approx)
150ml water
400ml full fat coconut milk
1 inch cubed fresh ginger
1 large garlic clove
1 teaspoon turmeric powder
1 teaspoon sea salt
Twist of black pepper
Handful chickpeas (pre-cooked)
Handful fresh parsley

How to make

1. Chop the sweet potato into cubes and put into a large soup pan.
2. Add the water and coconut milk and turn on the heat (once it comes to the boil, turn it down to a simmer).
3. In the meantime, peel and finely grate the ginger.
4. Crush the garlic clove.
5. Add the ginger, garlic, turmeric, salt and black pepper to the pan.
6. Cook for 15 to 20 minutes (or until you can easily pierce the sweet potato with a fork).
7. Pulse a hand blender through a few times - or simply mash through with a potato masher to break everything down into pieces and help everything meld together nicely.
8. Add the chickpeas and then heat through again for a minute (to warm the chickpeas up).
9. Finely chop the parsley and either mix in or use to garnish right at the end.

Creamy Mushroom Soup
with coconut & love

Heaven meets Earth! A heavenly creamy mushroom soup, blended to a creamy, satisfying perfection.

Serves: 4   Time: 20 minutes

Ingredients

2 leeks (medium sized)
500g brown mushrooms
Dash of olive or coconut oil
1 potato (medium sized)
500ml water
400ml full fat coconut milk
1 teaspoon sea salt (or to taste)
Black pepper (generous twist)
Small handful of parsley (optional)

How to make

1. Chop the leek into small pieces and then begin to sauté in a soup pan using the oil. Place on the lid and stir regularly over a couple of minutes.
2. In the meantime, chop the mushrooms into small pieces and then toss into the pan. Sauté along with the leeks. If the contents are too dry then add the smallest dash of water to loosen things up. Mix regularly over a couple of minutes.
3. Chop the potato into small pieces (use organic so that no peeling is required) and then toss into the pan.
4. Add the water, coconut milk, salt and pepper.
5. Allow the contents to cook for 15 minutes (10 minutes will suffice if the potato is chopped particularly small).
6. Use a hand blender to blend in the pan.
7. Add parsley to garnish (and mix in) if preferred.

"A single act of kindness throws out roots in all directions, and the roots spring up and make new trees."
Amelia Earhart

Easy Carrot Coconut Soup
with ginger & paprika

A simple soup, made with fresh ginger, carrot, smoked paprika, passata, coconut milk and potato.

Serves: 6   Time: 25 minutes

Ingredients

1 large onion
Dash of olive oil (to sauté onion)
7 carrots (medium to large size)
1 potato (medium sized)
800ml water
400ml passata
2 inches cubed fresh ginger
1 teaspoon sea salt
Big twist of black pepper
1 teaspoon smoked paprika
(optional but nice)
400ml coconut milk (canned)

How to make

1. Finely chop the onion and sauté in olive oil in a big pan for a couple of minutes.
2. Chop the carrot and potato into small cubes and then add to the pan along with the water and passata. Turn on the heat, bring the contents to boiling point and then turn down to simmer.
3. Peel and finely grate the ginger and add to the pan.
4. Add the sea salt, pepper and smoked paprika.
5. Cook for about 20 minutes with the lid on, stirring occasionally.
6. Add the coconut milk near the end of the cooking period.
7. When ready blend with a hand blender and serve.
8. This keeps for a few days in the fridge and also freezes really well.

Creamy Tomato Soup
with Sweet Potato, Rosemary & Lentils

Cream of tomato soup has never tasted so good. This is full of goodness, making a balanced, one-pot meal.

Serves: 3 to 4   Time: 25 minutes

Ingredients

- Two tablespoons fresh rosemary (finely chopped)
- 1 onion (medium/large)
- 1 large clove of garlic
- Dash of coconut oil
- 1 large sweet potato (500g approx)
- 625ml water
- 500ml passata
- 75g red lentils
- 1 heaped teaspoon dried parsley (or small handful of fresh)
- 1 teaspoon sea salt
- Big twist of black pepper
- 150ml coconut cream

How to make

1. Remove the stalks from your fresh rosemary. Finely chop the leaves as best as you can.
2. Peel and chop the onion.
3. Crush the garlic and remove the skin.
4. Sauté the onion and garlic with a dash of coconut oil for a couple of minutes in a pan.
5. In the meantime, chop your sweet potato into small cubes. Leave on the skin (for extra goodness), just chop off any bits that don't look good.
6. Add the water, passata, finely chopped rosemary, lentils and sweet potato to the pan, place on the lid and bring to the boil.
7. Allow to simmer for about 20 minutes.
8. Add the parsley, salt, black pepper and coconut cream near the end of the cooking time.
9. Blend until creamy (I use a hand blender to save on washing up).
10. Serve right away or over the next few days (the flavours keep dancing so it tastes even more delicious the longer you keep it).

Chilli Black Bean Soup

A nice spicy chilli black bean soup, with mushrooms, sweet potato, coconut, ginger and coriander leaves (cilantro). Warm, nurturing and nutritious.

Serves: 4   Time: 25 minutes

Ingredients

150g brown mushrooms
1 large onion
Dash of olive oil (or coconut oil)
1 large clove of garlic
1 fresh red chilli pepper
(medium spiced, about 5cm long)
500ml water
300ml passata
500g black beans (cooked)
1 inch fresh ginger
Big twist of black pepper
1 teaspoon sea salt
1 small sweet potato
200ml coconut milk
Big handful fresh coriander

How to make

1. Chop the mushrooms into pieces.
2. Chop the onion into tiny pieces.
3. Sauté the mushroom and onion in a pan with the oil for a couple of minutes.
4. Crush the garlic clove and finely chop the chilli pepper (with seeds) and add to the pan.
5. Add the water, passata and black beans to the pan and turn up the heat.
6. Once it comes to the boil, turn down the heat to simmer and pop the lid on.
7. Finely grate about an inch of fresh ginger and add to the pan along with a generous twist of black pepper and sea salt.
8. Leave the skin on the sweet potato and chop into very small cubes before adding to the pan.
9. Allow the contents to cook for at least 20 minutes.
10. When the soup is ready, add the coconut milk and heat through.
11. If it is not spicy enough then add extra black pepper (or a pinch of dried chilli powder perhaps).
12. Chop the fresh coriander, add to the pan, mix in and then it is ready to serve.

Creamy Cauliflower Soup
with coconut, nutmeg & rosemary

Grounding, earthy, fragrant. This tropical and celestial bowl of soup is a celebration of all things good.

Serves: 3 to 4   Time: 25 minutes

Ingredients

1 onion (medium sized)
Dash of oil
1 large potato
1 cauliflower (medium sized)
200ml water
Big sprig of fresh rosemary
400ml full fat coconut milk
1 teaspoon sea salt
½ teaspoon freshly grated nutmeg

How to make

1. Chop the onion into small pieces and sauté in a small amount of oil in your pan for a couple of minutes.
2. Chop the potato into small cubes (approximately 1cm cubed will work well).
3. Chop the cauliflower into small pieces.
4. Remove the stalk from the rosemary and finely chop the leaves. If you don't have fresh rosemary, then add up to a tablespoon of the dried stuff instead.
5. Add the cauliflower, potato, water, coconut milk, salt and chopped rosemary to the pan and bring to the boil.
6. Once boiling, turn down to a simmer and allow to cook for about 20 minutes.
7. Before the cooking period is over, finely grate the nutmeg and add to the pan.
8. When cooked, take a hand blender and pulse it through the soup. This is to partially blend it. We are looking for a 'part-blended' style, with plenty of chunks still left in there. If you don't have a hand blender, you could scoop out a couple of ladles full and then blend in a jug blender. Then mix back into the rest of the soup. Alternatively get a potato masher and simply mash through the soup.

Milky Matcha

This is my favourite healthy, vegan, milky matcha made with homemade walnut milk, maple syrup and vanilla. Delicious and nutritious.

Makes: 1 mug   Time: 3 minutes

Ingredients

300ml homemade walnut milk
1 teaspoon organic matcha powder
2 teaspoons maple syrup
1 teaspoon vanilla extract

How to make

1. See page 14 to learn how to make your own walnut milk. Alternatively, use any plant-based milk.
2. Heat the plant milk in a saucepan. Be careful not to over-boil it, as plant milks do sometimes separate if they are cooked too intensely. You need to gently heat it, bringing it to the point where bubbles start forming around the edge of the pan (and it should also be hot to touch if you dip your little finger in), but no more than that.
3. In the meantime, mix the matcha powder, maple syrup and vanilla in a mug until there are no lumps and everything is evenly mixed in.
4. Once the milk is hot, then pour into the mug with the matcha mix and rapidly stir. Enjoy immediately.

Hot Milky Turmeric Drink
with cardamom & ginger

A warming, milky, vegan turmeric drink with ginger, cardamom, coconut sugar and vanilla.

Makes: 1 mug   Time: 8 minutes

Ingredients

½ inch cubed fresh ginger
8 cardamom pods
100ml water
½ teaspoon ground turmeric (or use fresh)
Twist of black pepper
1 heaped teaspoon coconut sugar
1 teaspoon vanilla extract
300ml plant-based milk

How to make

1. Crush the fresh ginger with a pestle and mortar (or finely grate it).
2. Crush the cardamom pods - remove the pods and crush the seeds with a pestle and mortar (or use a quarter of a teaspoon of pre-ground cardamom).
3. Add the water, turmeric, ginger, cardamom, pepper, coconut sugar and vanilla to the pan and bring to the boil. Once boiling, turn the heat down to allow it to simmer for a couple of minutes. This draws out the flavour of the spices.
4. After two or three minutes add the plant milk. Cook until it starts to gently bubble around the edges. You don't want to heat it more than this if you can help it, because the milk might separate (if it does separate, then just add extra milk once served and it will be fine).
5. Strain with a tea strainer.
6. Serve immediately, adding extra milk if needed.

Mam's Pickled Daikon
HAWAIIAN STYLE

A picked daikon recipe from my Mam. A touch of coconut sugar, turmeric, black pepper and rice vinegar.

Time: 3 days or more to pickle

Ingredients

1 large daikon (about 25cm long)
1 tablespoon sea salt
125ml of water
2 tablespoons coconut sugar
125ml rice vinegar
½ teaspoon turmeric
½ teaspoon black pepper

How to make

1. Slice the daikon very thinly, either with a mandolin or sharp knife.
2. Put it in a bowl and mix in one tablespoon of sea salt. Leave for at least a couple of hours. The salt will help the liquid to release from the daikon.
3. In the meantime make the 'brine' liquid; put the water, coconut sugar, rice vinegar, ground turmeric and black pepper in a pan. Simmer the liquid for a few minutes, until the coconut sugar dissolves into the liquid. Once done, put this mixture to the side to cool for later.
4. When the daikon has been left for least two hours with the salt, use your hands to squeeze the water out. Discard the excess water.
5. Next, mix the squeezed daikon with the 'brine' liquid.
6. Put the daikon and liquid into a glass jar. Pop a lid on, then leave it in the fridge for at least three days. This allows the flavours to combine. If the daikon is not quite fully submerged under the brine, give the jar a shake a few times over the three days to allow everything to infuse evenly.
7. Store in the fridge. Use within a few weeks.

Daikon is essentially a huge, mild, white radish, known in other parts of the world as mooli, winter radish, Japanese radish, Chinese radish or oriental radish. It is said to be an ancient Mediterranean root vegetable, although it was brought to the East around 500 B.C. Daikon comes from two Japanese words: "dai" (large) and "kon" (root). As far as I can tell, it became popular in Hawaii when migrants brought it over from Japan. The Japanese tradition of pickling daikon has been enjoyed on the Hawaiian islands ever since.

It was Mam who inspired me originally in the kitchen, growing up as a Northumbrian lass in England – she always made the most of whatever we had available at the time. In fact, she still does, making delicious foods. I am always intrigued to find what new ingredients she is using, especially now she is in a far away lands. Fast forward to Hawaii where she's lived for many years now.

"Me & my Mam outside the health food store in Kauai, picking up some essentials, before a trip to the farmers market to get our daikon. I love this woman so much!"

Rosemary Roast Potatoes

This is a healthier roast potato with rosemary. Just enough oil to give them a nice little bit of crisp, without feeling drenched or saturated in the stuff.

Serves 6 to 8   Time: 60 minutes

Ingredients

1kg of organic potatoes
1 large sprig of fresh rosemary
Drizzle of olive oil
1 teaspoon sea salt
Big twist of black pepper

How to make

1. Make sure the potato skins are clean. Leave the skins on and then chop into even cubes of around 2cm cubed.
2. Finely chop the rosemary with a sharp heavy knife or a nut/seed grinder. If you are using dried rosemary, then it is probably already broken down in to tiny pieces.
3. Toss the potatoes in a bowl with rosemary, a dash of olive oil until evenly coated (I might only use a couple of teaspoons' worth of oil for this), salt and pepper.
4. Spread evenly on a baking tray or oven dish and then pop into a pre-heated oven on a high shelf for up to an hour. I use gas mark 7 (425°F/220°C). Roasting time will vary depending on whether you use a fan assisted oven or how efficient the oven is in general. You know they are ready when they start to look tanned. If your oven isn't very good at roasting, then pop under the grill for a few minutes at the end to tan them off (using a metal tray only - no glass under the grill).
5. Turn the potatoes a couple of times during the roasting period with a metal spatula.
6. Serve immediately and enjoy!

Easy Roasted Brussel Sprouts

Easy, simple roasted brussel sprouts make a fabulous side dish. This recipe uses a dash of oil, salt, pepper and a really hot oven. Perfect!

Serves: 6 to 8   Time: 35 minutes

Ingredients

500g organic brussel sprouts
A generous pinch of sea salt
A generous pinch of black pepper
A drizzle of olive oil (or coconut oil)

How to make

1. Cut any grubby bits off the sprouts.
2. Halve the sprouts (unless they are tiny ones, in which case leave them whole). Aim to get a tray full of sprouts that are approximately the same sort of size, to ensure even baking time.
3. Toss the chopped brussel sprouts in a bowl with salt, pepper and a drizzle of oil, until evenly coated.
4. Spread out on a baking tray.
5. Bake in a pre-heated oven at gas mark 7 (425°F/220°C) for at least 30 minutes or until baked.
6. Serve immediately.

Fresh Mango Chutney

This fresh chutney is popular with my guests on curry night, partnering perfectly with the baked pakoras on page 92. A sweet medley of warming spices.

Serves: 12   Time: 30 minutes

Ingredients

500g fresh mango
(about 2 large mangoes)
1 onion (medium sized)
Dash of olive oil (or coconut oil)
1 inch cubed fresh ginger
10 cardamom pods
50ml apple cider vinegar
1 teaspoon ground coriander
1 tablespoon coconut sugar
Pinch of sea salt
Twist of black pepper

How to make

1. Peel and chop the mango into chunks (compost the skin and seed).
2. Peel and chop the onion into chunks.
3. Sauté the onion for about three minutes in the oil.
4. In the meantime, grate your ginger with a fine grater.
5. Crush the cardamom pods with a pestle and mortar by removing the outer pods and crushing the seeds. Alternatively pop out the seeds and chop finely with a sharp heavy knife.
6. Add all ingredients to the pan and stir.
7. Heat until it starts to bubble and then reduce the heat to allow it to gently simmer. Stir the contents regularly over the next half an hour or so. The mango should eventually start to break down (which you can help by pushing downwards with a wooden spoon as it cooks and softens). All the ingredients should infuse and entwine together.
8. Once cooked, allow it to cool and then serve. If you aren't ready to use immediately then put in a clean glass jar with a lid and store in the fridge. This is usually fine for a couple of weeks (any longer then consider putting it in the freezer).

Onion Tamari Gravy

A crazy fast, easy gravy using tamari, onion powder, tapioca starch and water. Delicious, healthy, naturally gluten-free and vegan (as always).

Serves: 4   Time: 5 minutes

Ingredients

1 tablespoon onion powder

1 tablespoon (heaped) tapioca starch
(or tapioca flour/potato starch/corn starch)

300ml water

2 tablespoons tamari

Twist of black pepper (optional)

Extra sea salt to taste (optional)

How to make

1. Dissolve the tapioca starch and onion powder in a small amount of the cold water, by mixing with a spoon.
2. Add all of the ingredients into a saucepan and gently heat up.
3. Stir frequently and keep a close eye on it. As soon as it starts to get hot, it will go lumpy if you are not stirring it.
4. Keep stirring (especially when it starts to heat up). It should rapidly turn thick once it reaches boiling temperature. Again, keep stirring until it thickens nicely.
5. If for some reason it is not thick enough for you, take a small amount of tapioca starch, mix with a small amount of cold water and then mix that into the cooked gravy (this should thicken it up). Do not put the tapioca starch direct into the hot gravy without first mixing with cold water - because it will just turn to lumps (as it needs 'dissolving' in the water first).
6. Serve immediately or leave for a while in the pan and reheat again.

Notes

I often use tapioca starch as the thickening agent. However, you can substitute this for tapioca flour, corn flour, potato starch, corn starch, corn flour or arrowroot powder.

What is tamari?

Tamari is basically a fermented soya sauce, made without wheat. It is deeply rich, pleasantly salty and excellent as a gluten-free soya sauce.

Is there an alternative to tamari?

You can also use shoyu instead of tamari (which is a healthy alternative to soya sauce available in health food stores). Shoyu does however apparently contain some gluten, so be cautious if you have coeliac disease or have a gluten allergy. Although it is said that with a good fermented shoyu, there is practically no gluten left in it by the time it is bottled.

Simple Oatcake Wraps
Using a cast iron skillet

A delicious Staffordshire oatcake wrap using oats and water, with salt and pepper to season. Simple!

Makes: 4   Time: 10 minutes

Ingredients

150g ground oats
250ml water
Big pinch of sea salt
Big twist of black pepper

How to make

1. Either buy ground oats or grind them yourself. You can usually do this in a food processor, high powered blender or nut mill.
2. Mix the oats, water, salt and pepper together. Use a jug and a fork to 'whisk' these ingredients until evenly combined and without lumps.
3. Leave the mixture to settle for a few minutes (it will thicken in this time) and stir/whisk again. You need a batter mixture that is thick, yet easy to pour. If it is too thick then the oatcake wraps will likely crack. If it is too thin then it might do other weird stuff. The best way to learn this is by 'feel' and experience or trial and error. If your mixture is too thick, add a dash of water to thin; if it is too thin, then add a small amount of ground oats to it.
4. Heat your cast iron skillet until it is piping hot.
5. Pour about a quarter of your mixture onto the surface of the skillet and quickly smooth out with a flattish bottomed spoon.
6. Within a couple of minutes of being on the heat it will change consistency.
7. Use a metal or heat-proof spatula (known as a fish-slice in the UK) to gently tease the edges of the wrap. If it is going right, then the whole wrap should lift up effortlessly. If there is any resistance then leave it another minute. Once you peek underneath and see it starting to tan ever so slightly, you can flip it over and cook the other side for a minute or two.
8. When done, pop onto a cooling rack between the layers of a lint-free tea towel or between layers of kitchen paper. This is important for softening if you want to roll them up. Leave them for 10 to 15 minutes to soften enough so that you can roll them.
9. Stuff with your favourite dip and salad ingredients and enjoy for lunch. Alternatively, stuff with a bean recipe like my Spicy Black Bean One Pot (page 114) and create enchiladas. Or simply roll and use as an accompaniment to soup.

Easy Raspberry Chia Jam

Five ingredients. Free from nasty refined sugar. Meet my easy chia jam recipe with fresh raspberries. No cooking required.

Makes: 1 jar (300ml)   Time: 5 minutes

Ingredients

Juice of ½ a lemon
200g fresh raspberries
3 tablespoons of chia seeds
2 tablespoons coconut sugar
1 teaspoon vanilla extract

How to make

1. Juice the lemon and discard the rind.
2. Put the lemon juice, raspberries, chia seeds, coconut sugar and vanilla extract in a jug blender, food processor or a jug for hand blending.
3. Blend for about ten seconds or until everything is mixed together. It really is that easy.
4. Pop it into a clean jar with a lid.
5. Pop into the fridge.
6. The chia seeds will allow this 'jam' to thicken over about half an hour or more.
7. When ready take it out of the fridge, give it a stir.
8. This works well on crackers, toast, scones, on granola or mixed into porridge.
9. Serve as desired in the place of regular jam. Keeps for a few days in the fridge but also freezes well.

Oven-baked Flatbread

An easy gluten-free vegan flatbread recipe baked in the oven in just 20 minutes.

Makes: 8 triangles   Time: 30 minutes

Ingredients

75g rice flour
75g buckwheat flour
35g tapioca flour
35g potato starch or flour
1 teaspoon dried yeast
½ teaspoon sea salt
200ml tepid water

How to make

1. Mix all the flours together with the dried yeast and salt.
2. Add the tepid water and mix in thoroughly. You need a 'batter-like' consistency.
3. Pour mixture onto a parchment-lined baking tray.
4. Cover and leave in a warm place for at least half an hour. Leaving it in a warm place is essential to allow the yeast to work and give it a bit of a bread-like rise. I've left it for up to three hours before, which just creates even more of an airy rise.
5. Bake in an oven at gas mark 5 (190°C/375°F) for 20 minutes on the middle shelf.
6. It is normal that it will look a little cracked on top when you take it out.
7. Pop the tray onto a cooling rack to allow it to cool before slicing.
8. If you can't wait (like me) it does slice fine when warm, although it will slice slightly more easily if you let it cool.

Scottish Oatcakes

Scottish Oatcakes just don't get better than this. With oats and sunflower seeds, they are very popular with soup, dips and used as a snack.

Makes: 20   Time: 35 minutes

Ingredients

200g oatmeal (or ground rolled oats)
100g sunflower seeds (ground)
1 teaspoon sea salt
2 heaped teaspoons dried parsley
150ml water (approx)
Extra oatmeal (for rolling)
Dash of oil for baking tray

How to make

1. Turn your oven on to gas mark 7 (220°C/425°F).
2. Mix all of the dry ingredients together.
3. Add 150ml of water and mix into the dry ingredients thoroughly with your hands. You need to achieve a dough ball that holds together very firmly, but does not stick to your fingers. If the dough is too soggy then simply add more oatmeal until you get the right consistency.
4. Split the dough into two (this makes it easier to roll). Roll out onto an oatmeal dusted surface until it is about 3mm thick (about ¼ of an inch).
5. Cut with a cookie cutter (alternatively use the open top of a glass/jar or a sharp knife).
6. Place on an oven tray and then bake in your pre-heated oven between 20 and 25 minutes until they begin to gently tan.
7. Once baked, lift from the tray and place on a cooling rack. They should firm up nicely, with a crunch. If you want them softer take them out of the oven earlier.
8. Once cooled, they keep in an airtight container for about a week.

Soda Loaf Bread

With a perfect moistness, soft bite and delicious flavour, this gluten-free, vegan bread is free from yeast and gums. Serves nicely with soup.

Makes: 1 loaf   Time: 55 minutes

Ingredients

- 4 tablespoons ground flaxseed
- 175ml water
- 200g ground oats
- 100g millet flour
- 75g coconut flour
- 50g tapioca starch
- 1 teaspoon sea salt
- 1 teaspoon bicarbonate of soda
- 3 tablespoons coconut oil
- 1 teaspoon apple cider vinegar
- 250ml water

How to make

1. Mix the ground flaxseed with 175ml water and put to the side to thicken whilst you prepare the rest of the recipe.
2. Weigh and mix all the dry ingredients together.
3. Go back to the flax/water mix and whisk with a fork quickly to achieve a consistency like a beaten egg. Then add this to the dry ingredients.
4. Add the melted coconut oil, apple cider vinegar, 250ml of extra water and mix everything together thoroughly until it is evenly combined. Start with a spoon and then once it starts coming together use your hands. The dough should be slightly sticky (but not too sticky) and come together nicely into a firm ball.
5. Compress down evenly into a parchment-lined loaf tin. The loaf tin should be a 2lb (1kg) size otherwise a different depth will happen and adjusted baking time may be required.
6. Pop into the oven on a medium to high shelf at gas mark 5 (190°C/375°F) for 45 minutes.
7. Once baked, take out and cool on a cooling rack. Note: It may crumble if you slice it too soon. If you want really thin slices, then definitely let it cool down completely, or even refrigerate first.

So, here's the thing... gluten-free bread is never going to be the same as regular wheat bread. It's just not! You need to use completely different ingredients that dance together in a totally different way. However, that doesn't mean you can't have an absolutely delectable experience. We have to think out of the box a little and come to appreciate a new kind of experience.

Burgers, Slices & Bites

Spicy Bean Burgers

The art of making delicious, spicy bean burgers is so much fun. Using kidney beans, chickpeas and an assortment of warming spices, this one is a real treat.

Makes: 8 burgers   Time: 25 minutes

Ingredients

3 large garlic cloves
½ medium sized apple
300g chickpeas (cooked)
250g kidney beans (cooked)
6 tablespoons tomato puree
Small handful fresh parsley
1 tablespoon ground coriander
1 teaspoon ground cumin
¼ teaspoon chilli powder
¼ teaspoon white pepper
½ teaspoon ground cinnamon
½ teaspoon ground turmeric
4 tablespoons brown rice flour

How to make

1. Crush the garlic cloves.
2. Grate the apple.
3. Put the cooked (drained) chickpeas, kidney beans, grated apple and tomato puree into a large mixing bowl and mash everything together with a strong potato masher. Mashing will seriously help the binding process, although it's great to have a few textured chunks of half mashed chickpeas and beans in there too. So go for 'mostly' mashed with a few rustic chunks.
4. Finely chop the parsley (bear in mind that if the leaves are too big, they will hinder the binding process, so chop them as small as you can).
5. Add all of the spices, parsley and rice flour to the bowl and mix in, pressing down with the back of a metal spoon to make sure everything is evenly combined.
6. Form into patty shapes, firmly pressing together and place on a grill tray.
7. Grill on a medium heat for about 8 minutes on each side (or until tanned). Grilling time will depend on whether you have a gas or electric grill. The grilling process will help them hold together, although they will still be a little delicate until you turn them over, so take care during the turning process.

"A smile, a little bit of kindness, a loving heart, all have the power to change an entire life."

Beet Buddha Bowl Bites

These Buddha Bites are made with beets, sunflower seeds, hemp seed, ginger and parsley. Jam-packed full of plant-based goodness and love, love, love.

Makes: 15 to 20 balls   Time: 40 minutes

Ingredients

1 beet (tennis ball size approx)
1 small sweet potato
150g sunflower seeds (shelled)
1 small onion
1 large garlic clove
1 heaped teaspoon fresh ginger (finely grated)
1 small handful fresh parsley
50g hemp seeds (shelled)
2 heaped teaspoons ground coriander
½ teaspoon sea salt (or to taste)
Big pinch of black pepper

How to make

1. Grate the beetroot and sweet potato.
2. Grind the sunflower seeds.
3. Finely chop the onion.
4. Crush the garlic clove.
5. Finely grate the ginger.
6. Finely chop the parsley.
7. Mix all the ingredients together in a bowl, adding salt and pepper.
8. Next, you will need to the get the whole mixture to a 'squidgy' consistency. This will allow you to roll it into balls. You can use a food processor or hand blender to get the mixture to combine well. If you use a hand blender just press it downwards and pulse a few times throughout the mixture to get it to combine. If you have food processor just process between 10 and 30 seconds until it starts to squidge (before it turns to puree). If you have a Vitamix, use the tamper tool to blend whilst pressing down for 10 to 20 seconds, with a little loosening and scraping of the mixture (and repeat).
9. Pop in the oven at around gas mark 5 (190°C/375°F) and bake for 30 minutes.
10. Serve hot or leave to cool and enjoy over the next few days.

Baked Pakora

Hurrah for baked pakora. Veggies coated with a chickpea flour batter, baked, offer an amazing alternative to the deep-fried version of pakora.

Makes: 8 pieces   Time: 25 minutes

Ingredients

1 large carrot
1 small potato
1 inch cubed of ginger (2½cm cubed)
½ teaspoon sea salt
1 teaspoon onion powder
Twist of black pepper
½ teaspoon cumin seeds
1 heaped teaspoon curry powder
(or garam masala)
1 handful chopped parsley
(or coriander leaves)
75g chickpea flour
(garbanzo bean or gram flour)

How to make

1. Grate the carrot and potato (use organic and leave the skins on).
2. Grate the ginger using a fine grater.
3. Put all the ingredients into a mixing bowl and mix together thoroughly. This is easiest using your hands. Once everything starts to combine then 'squidge' and compress with your hands until everything is wonderfully melded together.
4. Line a baking tray with parchment paper.
5. Spoon dessert spoon-sized dollops onto the baking tray. Compress down slightly if you want them to be more like patties.
6. Bake in a preheated oven at gas mark 7 (220°C/425°F) for about 25 minutes.
7. Enjoy with chutney right away as a starter, a snack or as part of a curry night medley.
8. They work nicely cold the next day in a lunch box. Alternatively reheat under a grill for a few minutes.

"Making Pakora on Retreat in La Palma, Canary Islands"

Sweet Potato Seed Loaf

How about a top notch, versatile seed alternative to a nut roast? Using sunflower and pumpkin seeds this recipe is delicious and holds together to perfection.

Makes: 8 slices   Time: 60 minutes

Ingredients

- 300g sweet potato (approx)
- 200g sunflower seed
- 100g pumpkin seed
- 1 heaped teaspoon nutmeg (grated)
- Large handful fresh parsley
- 2 cloves of garlic
- 1 teaspoon sea salt
- Big twist of black pepper
- 1 tablespoon ground coriander

How to make

1. Peel the sweet potato and boil until you can pierce a fork through the chunks. If you cut into small cubes then it should only take around 10 minutes to cook.
2. Drain and mash the sweet potato.
3. Grind the sunflower and pumpkin seeds into a meal. It doesn't have to be super-fine.
4. Finely grate the nutmeg.
5. Finely chop the parsley.
6. Crush the garlic.
7. Mix all the ingredients together until evenly combined.
8. Line a loaf tin (a 1kg/2lb tin is the perfect size) with parchment paper and then pack the mixture very firmly down into the tin.
9. Pop into a pre-heated oven at gas mark 6 (200°C/400°F) and bake for 40 minutes. The appearance should start to change and it should looked tanned when baked.
10. Take out and slice with a sharp heavy knife and serve with gravy or tahini sauce.
11. Alternatively let it cool down and pop in the fridge and enjoy as cold slices for lunch. It keeps well for a few days in the fridge. If you want it warm again, then it reheats by 'toasting' under a grill.
12. This loaf freezes nicely, but do slice it first so that you can pull out only the amount you need.

Sweet Potato Hemp Burgers

High vibe, gluten-free vegan deliciousness beams from this easy sweet potato hemp burger. Made with pumpkin seeds and coconut for gorgeous flavour.

Makes: 8   Time: 25 minutes

Ingredients

100g hemp seeds (shelled)
100g pumpkin seeds
50g sunflower seeds
175g sweet potato
50g creamed coconut
1 teaspoon sea salt
Big twist of black pepper
½ teaspoon nutmeg (grated)
2 teaspoons onion powder
1 tablespoon ground coriander
1 teaspoon ground cumin

How to make

1. Grind the seeds to a meal in a food processor or blender. You are looking for a rustic meal (some fine, some coarse).
2. Peel and grate the sweet potato.
3. Grate your creamed coconut block (you can use coconut butter as an alternative). Be SURE not to use coconut cream by mistake as this will make it too soggy. Creamed coconut comes in a solid block (see page 165 for information on creamed coconut).
4. Add all the ingredients to the food processor and blend thoroughly, until everything combines. You should be able to press together with your fingers and have it stick together perfectly.
5. Shape into 8 to 10 patties.
6. You can pop them into the fridge for a while to firm up if you like, although it's not essential.
7. Pop them under the grill and tan on both sides (about 7 minutes each side, depending on your grill).
8. Enjoy immediately or eat cold at your leisure.

"How can I infuse a little more of the divine into everything I do?"

Easy Vegan Burgers
"Sunshine seed patties"

Delightfully delicious vegan seed patty burgers made with sunflower seed, pumpkin seed and carrot.

Makes: 12 patties   Time: 35 minutes

Ingredients

200g sunflower seeds
100g pumpkin seeds
300g carrots (approx 2 large)
1 large clove of garlic
1 teaspoon sea salt
Small handful dried parsley (or fresh)

How to make

1. Grind the seeds in a food processor until you get a rustic meal (some fine, some coarse).
2. Chop the carrots into small cubes and boil until you can pierce them easily with a fork (or they are a mashable consistency).
3. Either mash the carrots (if you don't mind a little bit of rustic-ness) or if you want them super-smooth then blend them to a puree with a food processor. It works both ways.
4. Crush the garlic or finely chop.
5. Put all the ingredients into a mixing bowl and mix thoroughly. This is easy if you use the back of a metal spoon and use a firm pressing motion, alternated with mixing. Mix until everything is thoroughly combined and sticks together really well.
6. Take dollops of the mix, (more or less depending on how big you want your patties) and shape into rounds, about 1½cm thick.
7. Pop any that you want to bake immediately onto a baking tray (lightly oiled or lined with parchment paper) and bake in a pre-heated oven at gas mark 6 (200°C/400°F) for about 25 minutes or until tanned.
8. Put any that you want to save into a container before cooking and freeze (but be sure to separate layers of the patties with parchment paper). You can also do the same and keep in the fridge for a few days if you aren't ready to cook them immediately.
9. Enjoy hot or cold as part of dinner, lunch, in a lunch box, picnic or as travel food.

We are talking about an incredibly versatile seed patty here. It can be served for dinner as part of a main meal, with salad for lunch. It makes an excellent picnic food, a nutritious lunch box snack and also travels well if you are hiking and in need of some delicious high-vibe sustenance to keep you going. It is also the sort of thing I might make as travel food when going on a long-haul flight. It is simply a delightful little nugget of nutrition!

Main Meals

Black Bean Vegan Tacos
with organic corn shells

Incredibly scrumptious. Organic corn taco shells, stuffed with a black bean, passata, coconut medley.

Makes: 5 tacos   Time: 30 minutes

Ingredients

- 1 onion (medium sized)
- Drizzle of coconut or olive oil
- 240g black beans (cooked)
- 200ml passata (salt free)
- 1 teaspoon sea salt
- Large twist of black pepper
- Pinch of chilli powder
- 1 heaped teaspoon ground coriander
- 30g creamed coconut (or coconut butter)
- Large handful of coriander leaves
- 5 taco shells (or equivalent)

How to make

1. Pre-heat your oven to gas mark 2 (150°C/300°F).
2. Peel and chop the onion.
3. Heat a drizzle of oil in a pan and then sauté the chopped onion for a couple of minutes.
4. Add the black beans and passata.
5. Give everything a stir and then pop on a lid. Stir regularly throughout the cooking period and keep replacing the lid.
6. Stir in the salt, pepper, chilli and ground coriander.
7. After about 10 minutes add the creamed coconut or coconut butter, allow to melt in and then turn off the heat.
8. Chop the coriander leaves and add these in last.
9. Stuff the taco shells with the mixture and then pop into the pre-heated oven.
10. Bake for 10 to 15 minutes (check the instructions on the taco packet for baking time guidelines).
11. Once baked, add a nice dollop of guacamole to each taco as you eat.
12. Serve immediately.

Chickpea Curry in 15 minutes

A 15 minute wonder food. Delectably delicious this chickpea curry is made with coconut, sweet potatoes and a whole lotta love.

Serves: 3 to 4   Time: 15 minutes

Ingredients

1 leek (medium sized)
200g mushrooms
½ tablespoon coconut oil
1 small sweet potato
¾ can coconut milk
200ml passata
¾ can chickpeas
1 teaspoon sea salt
1 heaped teaspoon curry powder (or garam masala)
½ inch fresh ginger
10 cardamom pods (optional)
Large handful of fresh basil leaves

How to make

1. Chop the leek and mushrooms into small pieces and sauté for a couple of minutes in the coconut oil.
2. Whilst the leek and mushrooms are cooking, slice the sweet potato into wafer-thin slices and then toss in the pan.
3. Be sure to keep replacing the lid on the pan, to keep the heat in and allow faster cooking. Simmer on a gentle heat.
4. Add the coconut milk, passata, chickpeas (strain the chickpeas if they are from a can) and add salt.
5. Add a heaped teaspoon of your favourite pre-blended curry powder or garam masala. Add more if you prefer a stronger taste.
6. Finely grate (or crush with pestle and mortar) the ginger and mix in.
7. Optional: crush cardamom seeds with pestle and mortar - being sure to remove the pods. You can add other favourite spices to the pan at this point (perhaps a bit of chilli or ground coriander etc. - not necessary, but nice to play with if you have time and desire).
8. This should all cook up within 15 minutes. Tear some basil leaves and mix them in right before serving (to retain their vibrancy and taste).

Lentil Cottage Pie

A filling feast with lentils and mashed potato that keeps everyone happy, whether vegan herbivore, omnivore or carnivore.

Serves: 4 to 6   Time: 90 minutes

Ingredients

Main part

250g mushrooms
1 leek (medium sized)
2 cloves garlic
Dash of coconut oil (or olive oil)
200g puy lentils
500ml water
2 tablespoons shoyu
Big twist of black pepper
1 tablespoon ground coriander
1 heaped teaspoon ground cinnamon
400ml passata (or 1 can tomatoes)
1 tablespoon coconut sugar
2 heaped teaspoons onion powder

Potato topping

600g potatoes
1 tablespoon onion powder
Twist of black pepper
1 teaspoon sea salt
125ml plant-based milk

How to make

1. Chop the mushrooms and leek into small pieces.
2. Crush the garlic.
3. Sauté the leek, mushroom and garlic gently for a few minutes in the oil.
4. Add all other ingredients for the 'main part'.
5. Bring the contents to the boil and then allow to simmer in the pot, stirring regularly for about 45 minutes. Alternatively, you can cook for about 25 minutes and then just leave it for a few hours once you've turned off the heat, in which case it will continue to cook in its own heat (I often like to do this and come back to it later).
6. In the meantime chop the potatoes into small cubes and boil for about 15 minutes (or until you can easily pierce with a fork).
7. Mash the potatoes with all other 'potato topping' ingredients.
8. Put the main part (that you previously cooked) into a casserole dish.
9. Add the mashed potato topping on top and smooth down with a knife, spoon or fork.
10. Pop in the oven and cook for about 45 minutes on gas mark 6 or 7 (200°C/400°F or 220°C/425°F).

Easy Ratatouille

This ratatouille recipe benefits from aubergine, courgette, red pepper, leek and parsley. Serves well as a stew with bread or with rice, potatoes or quinoa.

Serves: 2 to 4   Time: 25 minutes

Ingredients

- 1 aubergine (medium sized)
- 2 courgettes (medium sized)
- 1 leek (small/medium sized)
- 2 sweet red peppers
- 2 garlic cloves
- Coconut oil to sauté (or olive oil)
- 250ml passata unsalted
- Black Pepper (big twist)
- 1 teaspoon sea salt
- 1 heaped teaspoon coconut sugar
- 1 handful fresh parsley
- Mixed herbs (optional to taste)

How to make

1. Prepare the vegetables. Slice the aubergine, courgette, leek and red pepper into strips or slices.
2. Crush the garlic.
3. Drizzle some oil into a large pan and turn on the heat. Once the oil is hot, toss in the leeks for a couple of minutes and then toss in the aubergine, courgette, pepper and garlic.
4. Mix regularly over a couple of minutes.
5. Add the passata, pepper, salt and coconut sugar. Bring to the boil and then turn down and allow to simmer for about 15 minutes. Stir regularly, replacing the lid between stirs.
6. Chop the parsley and any other herbs you want to use. Toss into the pan and mix in near the end of the cooking period, once the vegetables all begin to soften.

Shepherds Pie
Black Bean & Mushroom Style

A satisfying shepherds pie with black beans, mushrooms, warming spices, tomato and coconut.

Serves: 4 to 6   Time: 60 minutes

Ingredients

Main part

1 courgette medium
200g chestnut mushrooms
75ml water
200ml passata
15 cardamom pods
400g cooked black beans
1 teaspoon heaped sweet paprika (or smoked paprika)
2 teaspoons ground coriander
1 teaspoon cinnamon
1 heaped teaspoon onion powder
1 teaspoon sea salt
Big pinch of black pepper
Pinch of chilli pepper (optional)
50g to 100g creamed coconut

Potato topping

600g potatoes
25g creamed coconut
½ teaspoon sea salt
Pinch of black pepper
75ml plant-based milk
Sprinkle of dried herbs (optional)

How to make

1. Chop the courgette and mushrooms into tiny pieces.
2. Add to a pan along with the water and passata and then gently bring to the boil. If you don't have passata you could half a tin of crushed tomatoes instead.
3. Once boiling, turn down to a gentle simmer. Keep the lid on, so that the moisture is retained. Stir regularly over the cooking period.
4. Crush the seeds from the cardamom pods and discard the outer pods.
5. Add the black beans and spices to the pan.
6. Allow to gently simmer for about 15 minutes.
7. Finely chop the creamed coconut block and pop it in right at the end, mixing thoroughly to melt.

In the meantime, the potatoes

1. Chop the potatoes into small cubes. Leave the skins on.
2. Put them in a pan with water and bring to the boil. They should cook within 15 minutes. They are ready when you can easily piece with a fork. Drain the water off the potatoes.
3. Finely chop or grate the creamed coconut block (unless it has melted already) and add to the potato. Mix it in right away to allow it to melt.
4. Add the salt, pepper and plant-based milk and mash thoroughly with a potato masher or fork.

Bring it all together

1. Put the 'main part' into a small casserole dish or oven dish.
2. Add the mashed potato to the top. Smooth it down evenly with a fork.
3. If you have some to hand add a light sprinkle of mixed dried herbs to the top.
4. Pop it in a pre-heated oven at gas mark 7 (220°C/425°F) for approximately 40 minutes.
5. Enjoy immediately (also keeps for a few days in the fridge).

Kind Earth Curry

Because 'amazing' just keeps getting better! This is an easy vegan sweet potato curry with coconut, chickpeas, tomato, fresh ginger, and curry powder.

Serves: 6   Time: 30 minutes

Ingredients

1 kg sweet potatoes (about 3 large)
1 heaped teaspoon ginger (finely grated)
300ml passata (or tinned tomatoes)
300ml water
1 tablespoon curry powder
1 teaspoon sea salt
200g chickpeas (pre-cooked)
100g creamed coconut
A handful of fresh basil or parsley

How to make

1. If the sweet potatoes are not organic, then peel them. If they are organic then feel free to leave the skins on (but cut off any bits that are gnarly).
2. Dice the sweet potatoes into small cubes (about half an inch cubed).
3. Finely grate about one heaped teaspoon of fresh ginger.
4. Put all the ingredients in a pan together (except for the creamed coconut and fresh herbs) and turn on the heat. Bring the pot to boiling point and then reduce to a simmer. Cook for about 20 minutes, stirring regularly. The curry is cooked when you can easily pierce the sweet potato with a fork.
5. Chop and add the creamed coconut and mix in until all is melted and stirred in evenly.
6. Chop or gently tear the herbs.
7. Toss in the fresh herbs right before serving.

Note: If you don't have creamed coconut, then use 100ml of coconut cream instead (and leave out 100ml of the water). If you want to use coconut milk then add about one 400ml can at the start of the recipe, but leave out all of the water.

"Sweet potato, tomato, and coconut. Right there! Marriage made in heaven."

Butter Bean Coconut Bake
with rosemary & nutmeg

A warmly welcoming vegan butter bean coconut bake with a gluten-free oat and sunflower seed topping.

Serves: 4   Time: 45 minutes

Ingredients

Main veggie part of the bake
1 small cauliflower
1 large onion
Drizzle of olive oil
150ml water
1 tablespoon rosemary (finely chopped)
1 teaspoon sea salt (or to taste)
Big twist of pepper
200g butter beans (pre-cooked)
100g creamed coconut

Extra sauce for the main part
1 heaped teaspoon tapioca starch (or corn flour)
1 heaped teaspoon onion powder
75ml water

Crumble topping
100g ground oats
100g ground sunflower seed
Sea salt (to taste)
Big twist of pepper
1 heaped teaspoon dried parsley
Water to bind

How to make

1. Chop cauliflower into small pieces.
2. Chop onion into small pieces.
3. Heat oil in large pan and then sauté the onion for a minute or two. Stirring occasionally but then replacing the lid.
4. Add the cauliflower to the pan and sauté for another couple of minutes. Stirring occasionally but then replacing the lid.
5. Add the water, stir ingredients and replace the lid to keep the moisture in and allow steaming of the cauliflower to happen.
6. Cook for about ten minutes to steam the cauliflower - stirring occasionally.
7. De-stalk and finely chop the rosemary.
8. Add the rosemary, salt, pepper, butter beans and mix in.
9. Chop the creamed coconut. (Note: Creamed coconut comes in a solid block form and melts on heating. It is delightfully rich and fragrant).
10. Add the chopped creamed coconut to the pan and allow it to melt in by stirring, replacing the lid between stirring to keep the moisture in.

Extra sauce for the main part

1. Once the cauliflower medley in part one has steamed and the coconut has been added, then make the extra sauce. Put the tapioca starch (or corn flour, if that is what you have) and onion powder in a small mixing bowl. Gradually add the 75ml of water to it and stir. If you add the water all at once, you'll just end up with lumps from the onion powder. So add a little, stir it, press out any lumps - add a little more water, repeat. When done add this to the pan and mix in. This will add more moisture/sauce to the whole thing and will thicken up really quickly upon mixing.
2. When done (the cauliflower should be steamed, with a nice bite - rather than over-cooked and mushy) put it into an oven-proof dish.

Crumble Topping

1. Grind the oats in a food processor.
2. Grind the sunflower seeds in a food processor.
3. Put the ground oats and seeds in a bowl and mix in salt, pepper and dried parsley.
4. Add a small amount of water to allow the crumble ingredients to bind together. Add slowly and in small amounts (otherwise, it will end up soggy). Rub the mixture together with your fingers to create a crumble topping.
5. Pop the topping on top and press down gently and evenly.
6. Pop the dish into a pre-heated oven at gas mark 6 (200°C/400°F) and bake for about 30 minutes, until the crumble is gently tanned on top.
7. Serve right away and enjoy. This crumble bake also works nicely cold the next day.

Bolognese (kinda)
Mushroom & Sweet Potato Style

A plant-based alternative to bolognese sauce. Serves with spaghetti, pasta, potatoes, quinoa or rice.

Serves: 4   Time: 25 minutes

Ingredients

- 1 onion (medium)
- 4 cloves of garlic
- Drizzle coconut oil (or olive oil)
- 1 stick celery
- 1 small sweet potato
- 400ml passata
- Large handful mushrooms (any sort)
- Large handful of parsley (fresh)
- Large sprig of fresh oregano
- 5 sage leaves
- ½ teaspoon sea salt (or to taste)
- Big twist of black pepper
- ½ teaspoon mixed dried Italian herbs
- 2 teaspoons coconut sugar

How to make

1. Chop the onions roughly.
2. Crush the garlic.
3. Sauté the onion and garlic in oil for a few minutes.
4. Chop the celery into small pieces and add to the pan.
5. Chop the sweet potato into small pieces and add to the pan. Keep stirring contents regularly.
6. Add the passata (tomato sauce or sieved/crushed tomatoes from a tin will also work).
7. Chop the mushrooms and add to pan.
8. Chop the parsley, oregano, sage leaves and add to the pan.
9. Add the salt, pepper, dried herbs and coconut sugar.
10. Mix the contents of the pan. Allow to simmer for about 20 minutes (or until the sweet potato is easily pierced with a fork and starting to fall apart).

"The best and most beautiful things in the world cannot be seen or touched, but must be felt in the heart."
Helen Keller

Spicy Black Bean One Pot

Nothing beats vegan comfort food. With warming spices, this black bean recipe serves well with potatoes, millet, quinoa or in a burrito wrap with rice.

Serves: 4 to 6   Time: 20 minutes

Ingredients

1 large red onion (or any colour)
Dash of oil (to sauté)
1 large garlic clove
100ml water
400g cooked black beans
300ml passata
10 cardamom pods
1 teaspoon sea salt
Twist of black pepper
1 teaspoon coconut sugar
2 teaspoons ground coriander
1 teaspoon ground cinnamon
½ teaspoon smoked paprika
Pinch of ground chilli
50g (¼ block) creamed coconut

How to make

1. Finely chop the onion.
2. Heat a dash of oil (I use coconut or olive oil) in a big pan and toss in the onion, stirring regularly for a couple of minutes.
3. Crush the garlic and toss in with the onion to sauté.
4. Add the water, black beans and passata and bring to the boil. Once it is boiling turn down the heat to simmer the contents.
5. Grind the cardamom seeds (after discarding the pods), with a pestle and mortar (or a sharp heavy knife) and add to the pan.
6. Add the salt, pepper, coconut sugar, coriander, cinnamon, smoked paprika and chilli and mix in.
7. Allow to cook for at least 15 minutes. Longer cooking is also great, if you have the time, as it allows the flavours to dance and infuse together even more.
8. Chop the creamed coconut (which comes in block form) and add near the end of the cooking period. Allow to melt in and infuse. If you don't have creamed coconut then use at least 100ml of coconut cream instead.
9. This serves right away or keeps for up to a week in the fridge (the flavours will also continue to develop as the days go by).

Eating a plant-based diet is good for the planet and our fellow animals. It also helps us to radiate with positivity, so that we can infuse a little bit more of the divine back into the world around us.

Butternut & Ginger Sauce
with rice noodles

15 minute dinners are the best. This one is a tasty, nutritious meal featuring squash, coconut and ginger.

Serves: 4   Time: 15 minutes

Ingredients

300g rice noodles
3 large handfuls frozen peas

Sauce ingredients

1 small butternut squash (between 800g & 1kg)
½ inch cubed fresh ginger
Big pinch sea salt
Big twist of black pepper
150ml coconut cream
125ml water (saved from water in cooking process)
2 teaspoons ground coriander

How to make

1. Put some water into a pan and turn on the heat, placing on the lid.
2. Peel and cube the squash into small pieces and then put straight into the pan to cook (make sure there is enough water to just cover the squash).
3. Get the ginger ready by peeling and chopping into small pieces (or grate with a fine grater).
4. In the meantime get another pan for the rice noodles. Put plenty of water in and bring it to the boil. Once it is boiling, pop the noodles in and turn it down to simmer. Rice noodles normally take about 5 minutes to cook, but check the instructions on your packet.
5. After the noodles have been cooking for a couple of minutes, pop in the frozen peas (turn the heat right back up again to boil). Once the noodles have cooked, strain them.
6. When the squash is cooked (if the chunks are small, this should be done in less than 10 minutes), strain off the water - but save about 125ml and add it back in right away. (I normally just guess this part to be honest).
7. Toss in the ginger, salt, pepper, coconut cream and ground coriander and mix for another minute, then blend until creamy. I find blending from a pan like this easiest with a hand blender (saves on washing up) although a jug blender will work well too.
8. Mix the sauce with the noodles & peas and serve immediately.

Golden Veggie Crumble Pie
with creamy coconut sauce

Creamy coconut sauce and golden veggies to fill your belly. Topped with a deliciously healthy crumble.

Serves: 4   Time: 45 minutes

Ingredients

1 large sweet potato
1 large carrot
1 onion (medium)
100g sweet corn kernels
A few mushrooms

Coconut sauce

100g creamed coconut
1 clove of garlic
1 heaped teaspoon tapioca starch
(or tapioca flour/corn flour)
1 teaspoon sea salt
200ml water

Crumble topping

100g oatmeal
50g shelled sunflower seeds
1 teaspoon sea salt
1 teaspoon ground coriander
Pinch of black pepper
3 to 4 tablespoons coconut oil

Optional crumble extras

Handful of fresh parsley
Sprig of fresh rosemary

How to make

1. Cut the sweet potato and carrots into cubes.
2. Slice the onion and dice the mushrooms.
3. Steam all the vegetables, except the sweetcorn, for about 10 minutes (or until just cooked).

Coconut Sauce

1. Chop the coconut block into pieces and place into a small saucepan. Note: if you live in a hot country or your kitchen is really warm then your coconut block may have already melted. In which case, you might find it easier to measure by popping the block into the fridge first, to harden, and then chopping the block in half.
2. Peel and crush or finely chop the cloves of garlic.
3. Put a heaped teaspoon of tapioca flour into a pan (alternatives to this include tapioca flour, corn flour or corn starch). Add the water and mix (to quickly allow the tapioca starch to dissolve in the water before heating). Add the coconut and garlic to the pan.
4. Put the pan onto a low heat and stir until the sauce thickens. Two things are happening here to create a creamy sauce: *1. the coconut will melt and 2. the tapioca starch will thicken it.* It is important that you keep stirring, otherwise it might go lumpy, so do keep an eye on it. Once it thickens, stir for another minute and then take off the heat. Note: If it isn't thick enough add a little extra tapioca starch (but be sure to dissolve it in a small amount of COLD water first - otherwise it will go lumpy).

Crumble Topping

1. Finely chop the rosemary and parsley (if opting to use them).
2. Mix all the topping ingredients together, first with a spoon. Then rub together between your thumb and the tips of your fingers to create a crumble like texture.

Bringing it all together

1. Pop the veggies into your oven-proof dish. For this quantity I use a 7 inch diameter oven dish that is 3 inches deep. You can use whatever you have available though (shallower and wider works fine too).
2. Finely chop any extra fresh rosemary and parsley that you want to add in. Put in with the veggies.
3. Mix the sauce in with the veggies.
4. Gently press down the veggie and sauce medley so that it is even and roughly flat.
5. Add the topping and press down gently to compact it.
6. Pop into a pre-heated oven at temperature gas mark 6 (200°C/400°F).
7. Bake for about 30 minutes (or until gently tanned on top).
8. Serve right away and enjoy!

Sweet Stuffed Pepper
with beet & sunflower seeds

A healthy medley of beets, sunflower seeds and coriander leaves. This serves perfectly with sauce.

Serves: 4   Time: 45 minutes

Ingredients

- 4 small to medium beetroot
- 175g hulled sunflower seeds
- 1 teaspoon sea salt
- 2 large garlic cloves
- 1 small red onion
- Large handful coriander leaves
- 2 large sweet bell peppers
- 2 tablespoons coconut cream (optional)
- 1 tablespoon tomato puree (optional)

How to make

1. Top and tail the beetroot and cut off any other tough bits.
2. Slice up the beetroot (1cm slices should be fine). Toss the slices on to a baking tray and bake on a medium to high heat for about a half hour. This softens them a little and helps to bring out a nice depth of flavour.
3. Grind the sunflower seeds in a food processor or nut mill until you get a rustic meal. It doesn't have to be finely ground although it should start to resemble a sort of rustic 'flour'.
4. Add the sea salt to the seeds.
5. Peel and crush or finely chop a couple of cloves of garlic.
6. Finely chop the small red onion.
7. Finely chop the coriander leaves.
8. Slice the sweet peppers down the middle and take out the seeds.
9. Once the beetroot has baked, blend it down. You can use a hand blender, jug blender or food processor for this.
10. Mix all the ingredients together in a bowl. As well as mixing, it is helpful to press downwards with the back of a spoon to get it all to combine and stick together. The moisture of the beetroot will help this.
11. Stuff the mixture into the peppers.
12. Pop into a preheated oven at gas mark 6 (400°F/200°C) for about 25 minutes. Make sure the peppers are soft(ish) and bake a little longer if needed.

A bit about beetroot

Hailed as a superfood, the humble beetroot (also known as beet) is a little treasure trove of health-affirming goodness.

Beets come in different colours (like white and orange), although they are most commonly known for their deep reddish/purple colour. The unique, earthy tap roots are the part that people most often eat, yet it is useful to know that the green leaves are totally edible and filled with beneficial nutrients too.

Beetroot…

- *is rich in nutrients*
- *has been shown to support healthy liver function*
- *helps to lower blood pressure*
- *has excellent antioxidant properties*

Winter Squash One Pot

This delicious infusion of warming spices and herbs makes for a tasty one pot vegan meal. Using squash and black beans creates a hearty, feel-good factor.

Serves: 2 to 3   Time: 25 minutes

Ingredients

800g winter squash
250ml water
1 teaspoon sea salt
200g black beans (cooked)
3 large garlic cloves
1 heaped tablespoon ground coriander
½ teaspoon freshly grated nutmeg
½ teaspoon ground cinnamon
3 tablespoons tomato puree
75g creamed coconut
1 handful parsley

How to make

1. Peel and dice the squash into cubes (no larger than 2cm or ¾ inch cubed).
2. Put the squash in a large pan along with the water, sea salt and black beans. Place the lid on to keep the heat in. Steam in the pan until soft.
3. Peel and crush the garlic and toss into the pan.
4. Add the ground coriander, freshly grated nutmeg, ground cinnamon, tomato puree and mix in.
5. About five minutes from the end of cooking time, chop the creamed coconut (which comes in block form) into small pieces and toss into the pan.
6. Put the lid back on, but mix regularly to encourage the melting process of the coconut.
7. Finely chop the parsley and mix in right at the end.

Crustless Vegan Quiche

Who needs a crust when you can go crustless! This quiche recipe uses chickpea flour creating simple goodness at its finest. Great hot or cold.

Serves: 4   Time: 55 minutes

Ingredients

- 150g mushrooms
- ½ sweet red bell pepper
- 1 small sweet potato (100g approx)
- Handful fresh parsley or coriander
- 250g chickpea flour (gram flour)
- 2 tablespoons tomato puree
- 1 tablespoon onion powder
- 1 tablespoon ground coriander
- 2 teaspoons ground sweet paprika
- 1 teaspoon sea salt
- 400ml water

How to make

1. Pre-heat your oven to gas mark 6 (200°C/400°F).
2. Chop the mushrooms and sweet bell pepper into small pieces.
3. Chop the sweet potato (including skin) into very small pieces (no larger than 1cm cubed). Small is important so that they bake evenly during the baking time.
4. Finely chop the parsley.
5. Measure the chickpea flour, tomato puree, onion powder, ground coriander, sweet paprika and salt into a mixing bowl.
6. Add the water to the mixing bowl slowly, pressing out any lumps that may have formed from the gram flour. Keep adding and mixing until all the water has been used up and you are left with a thick 'batter'.
7. Mix the mushrooms, red pepper, sweet potato and parsley into the batter.
8. Line an 8 inch (20cm) round baking dish with parchment paper cake liners (or alternatively, cut some parchment paper yourself). You could also omit the lining, although be warned, the mixture will probably stick to the dish.
9. Pop it into the pre-heated oven.
10. Bake for 40 - 50 minutes.

A note on baking times:

The final cooking time varies, depending on whether you are serving immediately or serving later.

- If you are serving immediately then allow to cook for about 50 minutes.
- If you are waiting a little while (say 15 minutes) before serving, then it will continue to cook in its own heat, while you are waiting, so 45 minutes is enough.
- If you are cooking and then allowing to completely cool down before serving, then it only needs 40 minutes in the oven.

Desserts

Mango Coconut Ice Cream

An easy vegan mango coconut milk ice cream with only three ingredients. Naturally sweetened as always.

Serves: 4   Time: 60 minutes (plus freezing)

Ingredients

100g dried mango
50g pitted dates
400ml full fat coconut milk (canned)

How to make

1. Soak the dried mango and the dates with the coconut milk, in a jug. You can do this for at least an hour, but overnight is also fine. You just need the dried fruits to soften enough to be blendable.
2. When ready, pop a hand blender in the jug that you've soaked everything in and blend the ingredients until creamy smooth. If you don't have a good hand blender use a jug blender instead.
3. Pour the mixture into a container. (I usually use a glass loaf tin, which is the ideal size for scooping out.)
4. Freeze for a few hours (or longer if you don't need it the same day).
5. When ready, take out of the freezer. This should be scoopable after being at room temperature for 10 to 20 minutes. If you can't wait, try running your ice cream scoop (or spoon) under hot water, dry it and the use it to scoop.

BLUEBERRY NICE CREAM

An easy blueberry blender ice cream recipe. Frozen banana, blueberries and vanilla extract. That's it!

Serves: 2 to 4   Time: 5 minutes

How to make

Ingredients

3 frozen bananas
100g frozen blueberries
1 teaspoon vanilla extract

1. Freeze the banana ahead of time by peeling and slicing.
2. Put all the ingredients into your food processor.
3. Pulse to start with. The frozen fruit might take a few attempts at blending before it begins to break down. After a little pulsing, take off the lid and scrape the ingredients down. Put the lid back on and pulse/blend again. Repeat the scraping down process a few times. This may take a few minutes and a little patience, but it's well worth it!
4. The nice cream will gradually begin to soften and blend and then will start to cream up. Once it starts to cream up, keep blending until you reach your desired consistency and serve.
5. Sprinkle on your favourite topping if desired (e.g. fruit, nuts, seeds, coconut flakes).

No Churn Cacao Ice Cream
with coconut milk

An easy ice cream with coconut milk, dates and cacao powder. Exceedingly delicious.

Serves: 5   Time: few hours (mostly soaking & freezing)

Ingredients

400ml full fat coconut milk (canned)
200g pitted dates
4 tablespoons cacao powder

How to make

1. Soak the dates in the coconut milk in a jug for at least 2 hours (or overnight). This makes the dates soft and easy to blend.
2. When ready add the cacao powder to the jug.
3. Use a hand blender (probably the easiest), jug blender or food processor to blend together until creamy smooth.
4. Pour into a container (I use a glass loaf tin for this) and then pop in the freezer.
5. Freeze for a few hours to get a perfect ice cream texture.
6. You can leave as long as you want. After a few hours, the ice cream will become harder - in which case, the best way to serve is to take out of the freezer and leave at room temperature until it is nicely scoopable (which is normally after about 20 minutes, depending on the temperature).

"No act of kindness, no matter how small, is ever wasted."

Aesop

Raw Superfood Brownies
with coconut and lucuma

Hands up who wants a raw, vegan, superfood brownie, using an alchemy of simple, nutritious ingredients!

Serves: 20   Time: 30 minutes

Ingredients

Main part

200g dates (pitted)
250g sunflower seeds
200g walnuts
200g raisins
1 heaped tablespoon ground cinnamon
6 tablespoons cacao power
2 tablespoons raw coconut oil (optional)
2 tablespoons maple syrup
2 teaspoons vanilla extract

Topping

200g coconut butter (or creamed coconut block)
3 tablespoons lucuma powder
1 tablespoon maple syrup

How to make

1. Soak the dates for an hour (or more) in advance if they are hard. Dates do vary a lot, so use your own judgement on this.
2. Grind the sunflower seeds in a food processor, into a rustic 'meal' (i.e. roughly ground, with some coarse chunks and some finer ground seeds).
3. Get a mixing bowl and mix the ground seeds, walnuts, dates, raisins, cinnamon, cacao powder, melted coconut oil, maple syrup and vanilla briefly with a spoon.
4. Take the mixture and blend in a food processor in batches. The number of batches will depend on the size and strength of your food processor. I use a large Magimix so two batches does the trick for me with this quantity, but if I use a different food processor, I'll need several batches.
5. Blend until it starts sticking together. Test with your finger and thumb. If you can compress the mixture and it sticks together nicely, it's perfect.
6. Line a container with parchment paper (I use one that is 24cm x 24cm or just under 10 inches x 10 inches).
7. Compact the mixture down really firmly into your parchment paper lined tin or container. Compacting firmly is important, as this is what holds it together. I either use my hands or the back of a metal spoon (or both). Spend some time with this until you are happy it is compressed as much as possible.

For the topping

1. Melt 200g of coconut butter (or one full block of creamed coconut). You can do this by filling a small pan with about 3cm (1 inch) of water, heating up the water on the stove and placing a heat-proof bowl over it. The coconut butter will melt. If you live in a hot country or your kitchen is hot, then it may have already melted ahead of time.
2. Once melted, add the lucuma powder and the maple syrup. This topping mixture might start to become 'claggy' at this stage. Just make sure everything is mixed in and it will be fine. See step 4 for more tips.
3. Spoon the topping on top of the brownie base. It may stick together in one big lump.
4. Spread it evenly, as best you can, until the whole brownie is evenly covered. If it is sticking together, USE YOUR HANDS rather than a spoon. The heat of your hands will warm the topping, making it softer and easier to spread evenly. Just press and smooth it. Magic. This may take a few minutes, so be patient.

Then chill before serving

1. Chill in the fridge for at least half an hour and then serve.
2. This recipe also freezes really well and is good for months if frozen.

Raw Hemp Seed Brownies

With dates to sweeten, sunflower seeds and cashew nuts for pazaz, these raw chocolate hemp brownies are surprisingly easy and insanely good.

Serves: 8   Time: 20 minutes

Ingredients

Main part

50g sunflower seeds (shelled)
100g cashew nuts
50g hemp seeds (shelled)
3 tablespoons cacao powder
200g dates (pitted)
1 teaspoon vanilla extract
1 to 2 tablespoons maple syrup or water
(optional if needed)

Topping

3 tablespoons raw coconut oil
3 tablespoons cacao powder
1 tablespoon maple syrup
1 tablespoon coconut sugar

How to make

1. Break down the sunflower seeds in a food processor until you get a coarse 'meal'.
2. Add the cashews, hemp seeds and cacao powder. Grind until you get a coarse meal. It doesn't have to be super-fine like flour, but needs to be fairly well ground (a few rustic chunks are fine).
3. Add the dates and vanilla and blend together.
4. The mixture may stick together (this depends on how moist your dates are, which varies from batch to batch). You need the mixture to stick together nicely when you press between your fingers. If it doesn't do that, then you will need to add extra moisture.
5. Add extra moisture by either using maple syrup or water. You might only need a TINY amount, so be very careful if adding it. Try a tablespoon first then blend again. Press between your fingers again to test and then add another little dash if required.
6. When you have the right consistency, press all of the mixture down very firmly into a parchment-lined container (I used my trusty 1kg/2lb loaf tin for this, although anything of that size will do).
7. Pop into the fridge or freezer and then make topping.
8. For the topping, melt the coconut oil (if not already melted).
9. Add the cacao, maple syrup and coconut sugar and mix together thoroughly.
10. Pour on top of the brownie and then pop in the fridge or freezer to set for 15 minutes.
11. When the topping has set, take out and slice up.
12. This keeps in the fridge for a week or the freezer for a couple of months.

Homemade Vegan Chocolate
with coconut sugar

A delicious, heavenly, easy vegan chocolate recipe made with coconut sugar to sweeten.

Yield: 4 bars   Time: 20 minutes

Ingredients

6 tablespoons cacao butter (chopped)
3 tablespoons coconut sugar
5 tablespoons cacao powder
1 teaspoon vanilla extract

How to make

1. Grind the coconut sugar down to a finer consistency (this 'finer' nature will allow it to dissipate evenly through the chocolate, ensuring that it doesn't sink to the bottom whilst the chocolate is setting).
2. Chop the cacao butter into fine pieces (this makes the process of melting much easier). You might also have cacao butter in 'drops' (in which case use heaped tablespoons to measure).
3. Get a saucepan and add about an inch of water. Place a heatproof glass bowl on top of the pan and heat the water on a low to medium heat.
4. Melt the cacao butter in the glass bowl, adding the coconut sugar and vanilla. Mix in regularly over the next few minutes.
5. When the cacao butter has melted add the cacao powder and mix in thoroughly.
6. Pour into a chocolate bar mould or a parchment paper lined container.
7. Set in the freezer (quickest) or in the fridge.
8. Pop out of your moulds when set and enjoy!

Questions to ask every day...

How can I be more loving?
How can I be more kind?

Orange Gingerbread Cake
Chocolate Style

A playful, chocolate orange gingerbread cake with fresh orange juice and fresh ginger.

Serves: 8   Time: 50 minutes

Ingredients

Wet ingredients

3 tablespoons fresh orange juice

1 heaped teaspoon orange peel
(finely grated loose)

1 heaped teaspoon ginger
(finely grated loose)

125ml rice syrup

75ml coconut oil

5 tablespoons water

1 large ripe banana

Dry ingredients

100g rice four

50g tapioca flour (or starch)

30g rolled oats (or ground oats)

4 tablespoons coconut sugar

4 tablespoons cacao powder

2 teaspoon ground cinnamon

1 teaspoon bicarbonate soda

Optional frosting

4 tablespoons raw coconut oil

1 heaped tablespoon coconut sugar

1 heaped tablespoon lucuma powder
(or cacao powder)

How to make

1. Juice a small fresh orange and use 3 tablespoons of the juice.
2. Use a fine grater to finely grate one loose heaped teaspoon of orange peel and one loose heaped teaspoon of fresh ginger.
3. Blend all of the ingredients from the 'wet ingredients' list together with either a hand blender or a jug blender (you could alternatively simply thoroughly mash the banana and mix by hand, but blending is best if you can for this stage).
4. Pre-heat your oven to gas mark 4 (175°C/350°F).
5. Put all of the ingredients on the 'dry ingredients' list into a mixing bowl. Mix and press out any lumps with the back of a metal spoon.
6. Mix the 'wet' and 'dry' together thoroughly.
7. Line a loaf tin (about 1kg/2lb size) with parchment paper.
8. Carefully pour and scrape your mixture into the parchment-lined tin and make sure it is distributed evenly.
9. Bake for 40 minutes on the middle shelf (if you have more than one shelf).
10. When baked, take out and pop onto a cooling rack. Let it cool down fully (especially if you are going to add the frosting).
11. When cooled you can add the frosting.

Make the frosting (optional)

1. Heat about 1 inch of water in a saucepan.
2. Pop the coconut oil, coconut sugar and lucuma powder into a bowl and place the bowl into (or over) the hot water to melt the ingredients gently. If the water is hot, this should happen quickly.
3. If you don't have lucuma powder for the frosting then use cacao powder instead.
4. Spoon the melted frosting on top of the cake. Allow it to fill any cracks (if there are any) on top of the cake and allow a little to trickle over the edges once the top is completely covered.
5. Chill in the fridge for ten minutes to set the frosting.

La Palma Island Banana Bread

A delightfully moist, gluten-free, vegan banana bread that holds together to absolute divine perfection. An excellent way to use up any ripe bananas.

Makes: 8 slices   Time: 50 minutes

Ingredients

Wet ingredients

3 ripe bananas (medium size)
75ml coconut oil
75ml rice syrup
3 tablespoons water
1 tablespoon ground chia seeds
1 tablespoon lemon juice

Dry ingredients

50g sunflower seeds (ground)
125g rice flour
50g tapioca flour
1 heaped tablespoon ground cinnamon
1 teaspoon bicarbonate of soda

How to make

1. Mix all the 'wet ingredients' together with a hand blender or jug blender and put them aside for a few minutes.
2. Pre-heat the oven to gas mark 5 (190°C/375°F).
3. Line a loaf tin with parchment paper (a 1kg or 2lb loaf tin is ideal for this recipe).
4. Grind the sunflower seeds using a nut mill or food processor. It doesn't need to be a super-fine sunflower seed 'flour' although it does need to be ground down fairly well.
5. Mix all the 'dry ingredients' together.
6. Add the wet and dry together. Quickly and thoroughly mix. When combined press down into the parchment-lined loaf tin.
7. Pop into your pre-heated oven and bake for 40 minutes (give-or-take with this timing, depending on your oven). It should feel firm to press and be tanned on top.
8. When ready, take out of the oven. Take the loaf out of the tin (carefully pull out using the parchment paper) and place on a cooling tray so that the air can breathe underneath the loaf as it cools.
9. When cooled, slice up and serve.
10. It should keep for two or three days, although it will probably get a little drier as the days go by. Putting it in the fridge will firm it up (I prefer to serve at room temperature for optimal consistency).

Christmas Sweet Mince Pies

Seriously the best homemade gluten-free sweet mince pies ever. Sweetened with raisins and a dash of maple syrup. A British favourite.

Makes: 12   Time: 30 minutes

Ingredients

Sweet mince pie filling

1 teaspoon lemon zest (loose)
1 lemon (medium sized)
150g raisins
2 tablespoons maple syrup
1 tablespoon water
½ teaspoon nutmeg (freshly grated)
1 teaspoon cinnamon
1 tablespoon fresh ginger (grated)

Sweet mince pie pastry

100g rice flour
100g tapioca flour (or tapioca starch)
2 tablespoons ground flaxseed
4 tablespoons coconut oil
4 tablespoons maple syrup

How to make

Making the vegan mincemeat filling

Start by making and soaking the sweet mince in a bowl overnight (or for at least three hours) as follows...

1. Grate about 1 teaspoon of lemon zest, using a fine grater.
2. Juice the lemon.
3. Mix all the 'sweet mince filling' ingredients together in a bowl and soak overnight (or for at least 3 hours). Mix in several times during the soak period if you remember, as this helps the medley combine.
4. Once soaked, the raisins will be plumper as they should have absorbed most of the soak liquid.
5. Next, pulse the mixture with a hand blender a few times or use a regular jug blender, to create a rustic sweet mince 'mush'.

Making the mince pies

1. You will need a shallow cupcake tin for 12 cupcakes.
2. Make sure the coconut oil is warm and melted.
3. Mix all of the pastry ingredients together. Use a spoon at first and then work with your hands. If your kitchen is cold, then the coconut oil may solidify, in which case, the warmth of your hands will help to keep it soft and pliable. After a couple of minutes you should get a nice dough ball.
4. Sprinkle rice flour on your rolling surface and sprinkle a little rice flour on top of your dough to stop it sticking to the surface or to the rolling pin.

5. Roll the pasty with a rolling pin (or a large glass jar) and keep turning/rolling (which helps it roll evenly) until it is about 4mm thick. If the pastry starts falling slightly apart as it gets thinner, then just push it back together. I tend to use a super-thin spatula or frying pan slice to slide under it and stop it sticking to the kitchen worktop at this stage.
6. Cut out 12 circles with a cookie cutter (or the open end of a drinking glass works too).
7. Gently push each circle into the cupcake tin indents.
8. Roll the remaining pastry and cut out 12 stars with it.
9. Share the sweet vegan mincemeat mix between each pie and spread it fairly evenly.
10. Put a star on top of each pie.
11. Bake in a preheated oven at gas mark 5 (180°C/375°F) for about 20 minutes.
12. Once baked, allow to cool and serve. They should keep for a good few days in the kitchen or in the fridge too.

TIP: If you have spare pastry just roll it out and bake along side the mince pies and enjoy as a cookie!

Jam Tarts

Be prepared for some seriously good, *vegan jam tarts. Made with a melt-in-the-mouth shortbread type pastry, this is a whole new level of deliciousness.*

Makes: 12   Time: 30 minutes

Ingredients

4 tablespoons coconut oil
100g rice flour
100g tapioca flour (or tapioca starch)
2 tablespoons ground flaxseed
1 teaspoon vanilla extract
4 tablespoons maple syrup
200ml sugar-free jam

How to make

1. You will need a shallow cupcake tin with 12 cupcake indents.
2. Make sure the coconut oil is warm and melted.
3. Mix all of the ingredients together, except the jam. Use a spoon at first and then work with your hands. If your kitchen is cold, then the coconut oil may solidify, in which case, the warmth of your hands will help to keep it soft and pliable. After a couple of minutes you should get a nice dough ball.
4. Sprinkle rice flour on your rolling surface and sprinkle a little rice flour on top of your dough to stop sticking to the surface or to the rolling pin.
5. Roll the pasty with a rolling pin (or a large glass jar) and keep turning/rolling (which helps it roll evenly) until it is about 3 or 4mm thick. If the pastry starts falling slightly apart as it gets thinner, then just push it back together. I tend to use a super-thin spatula or frying pan slice to slide under it and stop it sticking to the kitchen worktop.
6. Cut out 12 circles with a cookie cutter (or the open end of a drinking glass will work too).
7. Gently push each circle into the cupcake tin.
8. Put a heaped teaspoon sized dollop of jam into each pastry and spread it evenly.
9. Bake in a preheated oven gas mark 5 (375°F/180°C) for about 20 minutes.
10. Once baked, allow to cool and serve. They should freeze well if you don't want to eat them immediately. They should also keep for at least a good few days in the kitchen or in the fridge too.

Raw Strawberry Cheesecake

If heaven was a pie this might just be it! This is a divine raw vegan strawberry cheesecake recipe.

Makes: 10 slices
Time: 45 minutes (plus freezing/soaking)

Ingredients

Base
150g almonds
100g pitted dates
1 teaspoon vanilla extract

Topping
125g cashew nuts
1 heaped teaspoon lemon rind (finely grated)
100g creamed coconut block
300g fresh strawberries (or frozen)
1 heaped tablespoon coconut sugar
1 teaspoon vanilla extract

Optional chocolate drizzle
1 tablespoon of chocolate (melted)

How to make

Ahead of time, soak the cashew nuts overnight (or for at least 2 hours).

Make the base

1. Grind the almonds in a food processor until you get a coarse meal (some powdered and some a little rustic and chunky is fine).
2. Add the dates and vanilla and blend until everything evenly combines.
3. Pack into a parchment-lined tin firmly (a tin sized 21cm/8 inches in diameter works well) and then put into the fridge or freezer whilst you prepare the topping.

Make the topping

1. Please note that we are using "creamed coconut" in this recipe or coconut butter (see page 165 for info on what creamed coconut is) NOT coconut cream (which is different). Blend all the topping ingredients together.
2. Grate your lemon rind with a fine grater.
3. Drain the soaked cashews thoroughly.
4. Pour onto the base and spread evenly.
5. Pop it into the freezer for a few hours to firm up.
6. When frozen, drizzle some melted chocolate on top if you want to.

How to serve

This serves right out of the freezer as a frozen dessert (very firm), although it works best if you allow it to acclimatise to room temperature and soften for at least 10 to 15 minutes before serving. The longer you leave it out, the more it softens (although soft can also be incredibly delicious and welcomed too, so explore and find out what you prefer).

Simple Chocolate Cupcakes

An easy, gluten-free vegan cupcake, sweetened naturally with maple syrup and banana. Delicious - it also freezes nicely too.

Makes: 12   Time: 30 minutes

Ingredients

Wet ingredients

1 banana (medium sized)
100ml maple syrup
100ml water
100ml coconut oil (melted)
1 teaspoon apple cider vinegar
1 teaspoon vanilla extract

Dry ingredients

2 heaped tablespoons (chopped) homemade vegan chocolate
100g rice flour
50g tapioca flour (or tapioca starch)
50g cocoa powder
1 teaspoon bicarbonate of soda

How to make

1. Pre-heat your oven to gas mark 5 (190°C/375°F).
2. Prepare a cupcake tin with space for 12 cupcakes and pop a cupcake case into each one.
3. Blend all the 'wet ingredients' together with a hand blender. Be sure to melt the coconut oil first if it needs to be melted, by placing the jar on a warm windowsill ahead of time, or popping the jar into a pan with hot water.
4. Chop up your homemade chocolate into small chips.
5. Mix the other dry ingredients together, pressing out any lumps and then adding your chopped chocolate.
6. Mix the wet and dry ingredients together. This should quickly turn into a thick batter.
7. Evenly distribute the batter into the cupcake cases (I find this easiest using two teaspoons).
8. Bake in the oven for about 18 minutes (more or less, depending on your oven).
9. When done take out and allow to cool for a few minutes in the tin, before moving each one to a cooling rack.
10. Enjoy the same day when they've cooled. Store at normal room temperature in a container. If you want to put them in the fridge then be aware that they will go quite firm and are best served at room temperature. They keep for a couple of days and also freeze nicely.

"I've learned that people will forget what you said, people will forget what you did, but people will never forget how you made them feel."
Maya Angelou

Sweet Potato Cacao Cake
WITH AVOCADO CHOCOLATE FROSTING

A scrumptious, gluten-free cake. Naturally sweetened along with a tasty avocado chocolate frosting.

Makes: 8 slices   Time: 40 minutes

Ingredients

Wet ingredients

175g sweet potato
1 teaspoon apple cider vinegar
2 teaspoons vanilla extract
100ml coconut oil (melted)
6 tablespoons water
3 tablespoons maple syrup
2 tablespoons ground chia seeds

Dry ingredients

100g rice flour
50g ground oats
50g tapioca flour
1 teaspoon bicarbonate of soda
5 tablespoons cacao powder
1 tablespoon of ground cinnamon
6 tablespoon coconut sugar
¼ teaspoon nutmeg (freshly grated)

Frosting

100g dates (pitted)
½ medium avocado
1 teaspoon vanilla extract
3 tablespoons of cacao powder

How to make

1. Peel the sweet potato first. You need one smallish sweet potato and are looking for about 175g (when peeled) - a little more or less is fine.
2. Boil the sweet potato until you can gently pierce a fork though. If you chop into small chunks then this shouldn't take more than 10 minutes. When cooked, thoroughly drain with a sieve or colander.
3. Put all the ingredients 'wet ingredients' into a jug and blend until smooth.
4. Now is a good time to turn your oven on to pre-heat it to gas mark 4 (175°C/350°F).
5. Mix all the 'dry ingredients' together in a bowl.
6. Add the blended 'wet ingredients' to the bowl and mix together thoroughly.
7. Line a loaf tin (1kg/2lb loaf tin) with parchment paper and put the cake mix in.
8. Pop into the oven for 40 minutes.
9. When baked put the cake tin onto a cooling rack. It can be fragile until it has cooled down, so it helps to let it cool down in the tin. Be very careful when taking out.

To make the frosting

Blend all the 'frosting' ingredients together to form a puree. Make sure your dates are pitted and if they aren't soft then be sure to soak them ahead of time. When the cake has cooled down, gently spread the frosting on it with a knife.

Chocolate Bodhi Bars

Because we all love a healthy chocolate bars. This is a nut and date layer covered with a soft homemade chocolate and then sprinkled with almonds. Yum!

Makes: 6 bars   Time: 20 minutes

Ingredients

Bottom layer

50g almonds
50g walnuts
100g dates pitted (about 14 dates)
1 teaspoon vanilla extract

Top chocolate layer

3 tablespoons cacao butter (approx)
1 tablespoon coconut oil
2 tablespoons maple syrup
3 tablespoons cacao powder
½ teaspoon vanilla extract

Extra topping

12 almonds

How to make

Bottom layer

1. Grind the almonds in a food processor into a rustic 'meal'.
2. Add the walnuts and grind for a few seconds more.
3. Add the dates and vanilla, then blend until everything blends together nicely. Rustic chunks are fine as long as everything has broken down and is binding well.
4. Press these ingredients very firmly into a parchment lined loaf tin (or use any container and line with parchment paper). A 1kg (2 lb) loaf tin is ideal for size.

Top chocolate layer

1. Get a small saucepan and a heatproof glass bowl that fits in the pan. Heat about an inch of water in the pan.
2. Put the cacao butter in the heatproof bowl and allow it to gently melt.
3. Add the coconut oil to melt it and then add the maple syrup.
4. Mix in the cacao powder and vanilla.
5. Pour this over the bottom layer you made before.

Extra topping

Chop almonds into pieces with a sharp heavy knife (or roughly crush with a pestle and mortar). Sprinkle chopped/crushed almonds onto the chocolate before the chocolate sets.

Setting the chocolate

Pop the tin into the freezer to set (a fridge will work too but takes a little longer). The chocolate should set firmly and be ready to slice within 20 minutes.

Raw Mango Cheesecake
WITH RASPBERRY CHIA SAUCE

No-bake and naturally gluten-free. Sweetened only with fresh fruits and a dash of maple syrup.

Makes: 8 slices   Time: 10 mins (plus soaking/freezing)

Ingredients

Base layer

150g almonds
1 teaspoon vanilla extract
2 tablespoons maple syrup

Topping

50g creamed coconut
150g fresh mango chopped
150g cashew nuts
1 teaspoon vanilla extract
1 tablespoon maple syrup
Juice of ½ lemon
½ teaspoon lemon rind (finely grated)

Sauce (optional)

100g raspberries
1 tablespoon maple syrup
2 tablespoons chia seeds
7 tablespoons water

How to make

In advance: soak the cashew nuts in water for at least an hour (several hours or even overnight is fine too). Drain them before use (you will use them in the top layer).

Base layer

1. Use a food processor to grind the almonds to a meal. It's okay if this meal is a little rustic with tiny pieces, rather than finely ground.
2. Add the vanilla extract and maple syrup until everything comes together. This mixture should stick together nicely between your fingers when pressed.
3. Line a round tin or container with parchment paper and compact the mixture down very firmly to create a 'crust' base layer. Pop it in the fridge whilst you make the next layer.

Topping

1. Finely chop the creamed coconut. Pop all of the ingredients into the food processor and blend thoroughly until there are no pieces and everything is evenly combined.
2. Spread the topping evenly over the base.
3. Pop it in the freezer for at least an hour. If you have time, then leave it for a few hours so it firms up really well and slices nicely.

Sauce (optional)

1. Blend all the sauce ingredients together and pop in the fridge or simply leave on your kitchen counter.
2. The chia seeds will start to expand and act as a gelling agent over the next half hour. Stir two or three times during this period.

To serve

- Take out of the freezer, slice with a sharp, heavy knife.
- Pour or dollop on some of the raspberry chia sauce if desired.
- Allow about 30 minutes before eating (to soften it a little).
- This keeps well for a couple of months in the freezer.

Vanilla Shortbread Cookies

A delicious crunchy shortbread cookie recipe made with only six ingredients. Naturally sweetened with maple syrup and benefiting from ground flaxseed.

Makes: 10 cookies   Time: 20 minutes

Ingredients

- 100g brown rice flour
- 100g tapioca flour (or tapioca starch or cassava flour)
- 2 tablespoons ground flaxseed
- 4 tablespoons coconut oil
- 2 teaspoons vanilla extract
- 4 tablespoons maple syrup
- Extra sprinkle of rice flour to roll with

How to make

1. In a bowl, mix together the rice flour, tapioca flour and flaxseed.
2. Melt the coconut oil.
3. Add the coconut oil, vanilla extract and maple syrup to the bowl and mix in thoroughly with a spoon. Once it starts bind I like to use my hands to bring it together into a dough ball.
4. Squash together and then sprinkle a little rice flour on your work surface.
5. Press the mixture down and then start rolling with a rolling pin. The mixture might start to fall apart (this is normal). Just push back together any parts that fall away.
6. Roll until it becomes about ½cm (¼ inch) thick.
7. Cut out your cookies. You could use a knife to cut into squares or use a cookie cutter (or the top of a drinking glass). Slide a cake slice or a knife under each cookie and pop them onto a baking tray.
8. Pop into a pre-heated oven at gas mark 4 (350°F/180°C) for between 12 and 15 minutes (depending on your oven).
9. They'll stay light in colour (if they tan, then they are probably over cooked). Once baked pop them on to a cooling rack.
10. Serve once cooled.

Vegan Chocolate Cake

This recipe uses coconut sugar and banana to sweeten. Flaxseed, gluten-free oatmeal, rice flour and tapioca flour all make for a fabulous treat.

Makes: 8 slices   Time: 50 minutes

Ingredients

Wet ingredients

2 tablespoons flaxseed
6 tablespoons water
125ml coconut oil
2 ripe bananas (medium sized)
1 teaspoon apple cider vinegar
2 teaspoons vanilla extract

Dry ingredients

100g rice flour
50g ground oats
50g tapioca flour or starch
1 teaspoon bicarbonate of soda
5 tablespoons cacao powder
1 tablespoon ground cinnamon
6 tablespoons coconut sugar

How to make

1. Mix the flaxseed and water together and leave to thicken.
2. Put the rest of the 'wet ingredients' into a jug. Add the flaxseed mixture last, then blend with a hand blender (or jug blender) until creamy.
3. Mix all 'dry ingredients' in a bowl.
4. Fold the wet ingredients into the dry ingredients.
5. Mix thoroughly and then whip rapidly with a spoon briefly, to get some air into the mixture.
6. Pour into a parchment-lined 1kg (2lb) loaf tin.
7. Pop into a middle/high shelf in an oven pre-heated to gas mark 4 (350°F/180°C). Everyone's oven is different, so use your intuition at this point.
8. Bake for 40 minutes (works well for most ovens).
9. Take out and allow to fully cool on a cooling rack.
10. It's normal that the top will crack a little.
11. Once cool, slice and enjoy. It keeps nicely in an airtight container at room temperature for a few days and also freezes well.

Blackberry & Apple Crumble

An apple & blackberry crumble using a wonderful oat, cinnamon topping.

Serves: 6   Time: 45 minutes

Ingredients

Filling

6 sweet apples (medium sized)
Big handful blackberries
2 to 3 tablespoons water
2 teaspoons ground cinnamon
2 tablespoons coconut sugar
1 teaspoon vanilla extract

Topping

2 tablespoons coconut oil
50g nuts or seeds (ground)
150g oatmeal (ground oats)
3 tablespoons rice syrup (or maple)
1 teaspoon almond extract
1 teaspoon cinnamon

How to make

1. Chop the apples into small cubes.
2. Cook the apples, with the blackberries and 2 to 3 tablespoons of water, in a pan for about 10 minutes. The small amount of water will be enough to help the cooking process (without creating excessive amounts of juice). Stir regularly, but keep replacing the lid between stirs. At the end of the cooking period, mix in the cinnamon, coconut sugar and vanilla.
3. In the meantime make the crumble topping.
4. Melt the coconut oil and then mix all topping ingredients together until you create a crumble. This crumble should stick together when you press firmly with your fingers - that's when you know it is ready.
5. Put the fruit filling in a baking dish and top with the crumble. Pat the crumble down gently to encourage a certain amount of 'holding together'.
6. Pop into a pre-heated oven at gas mark 5 (375°F/190°C) and bake for about 30 minutes.
7. Serve hot or cold.

What's in the Kind Earth pantry?

Let's take a peek and see what I keep in my pantry. I hope this section inspires you to have healthy, nutritious ingredients and foods to hand in your kitchen. Having a good stock of essentials available ensures that whenever you feel inspired, you can magic something up to eat. It also means that if you suddenly crave a snacky treat, you have healthy choices available to you, so that you'll never need to reach for junk foods again.

Always buy as ethically as possible looking for fair-trade brands, organic, minimal packaging or buy from package free shops. If you have local options available, then always go for those and see what you can create.

Seeds & Nuts

√ *Excellent nutritional profiles for essential fats, proteins and minerals*
√ *Great for snacking*

Choose a couple or several of your favourite nuts and seeds to have on hand for snacking or adding to granola, sprinkling on breakfast, making spreads, for nut milks or using as the base for nut and seed loaves or burgers. Always go for local options if you have them. We can forage hazelnuts and walnuts in Britain in the autumn, so I favour those. Almonds were my first choice when I spent a few months in the Canary Islands.

Walnuts
Very oily and high in omega 3 essential fats. Walnuts breakdown and blend well even without having to soak ahead of time.

Almonds
Particularly high in calcium with a lovely taste.

Sunflower Seeds
Great for snacking and using in lots of my recipes.

Pumpkin Seeds
Excellent for the mineral zinc. Good source of tryptophan (an amino acid) which converts to serotonin (a natural relaxant and mood balancer). Pumpkin seeds work well soaked for pâtés or dried and ground for bake toppings.

Hemp Seeds
Hemp seeds have nature's perfect balance of omega 3 to omega 6 ratio. They are good for essential fats and are a complete protein. Hemp seeds are great in superfood sweet treats and energy balls. They make an excellent plant-based milk and have a tonne of health benefits.

Chia Seeds
1 tablespoon of chia provides more calcium than a cup of cow's milk; more omega 3 than a piece of salmon and more antioxidants than a handful of blueberries. Chia seeds are an excellent thickening agent for smoothie bowls and work well in superfood sweet treats.

Flaxseeds
Top points for flaxseeds, for their impressive levels of omega 3 essential fats. Flaxseeds work well in baked foods, granola or in raw superfood sweet treats. They are best used ground and stored in a fridge or freezer.

Natural Sweeteners & Dried Fruits

√ *Dried fruits make excellent quick snacks*
√ *Much healthier than regular refined sugar*

Refined sugar has a lot of its nutrients stripped out which can wreak havoc on the blood sugar levels since the nutrients are required to help properly metabolise the sugar. Here are some alternatives...

Dates
Very snackable, nutritious little gems. Great sweeteners for superfood treats, energy balls and cake 'frostings'. They go well in plant-based milks for subtle (or not so subtle) sweetening.

Raisins
Great to add to salad, muesli and granola. Raisins have a high boron content, which is important for activating vitamin D, which in turn helps us to absorb calcium more efficiently.

Coconut Sugar
Low on the glycemic index compared to refined sugar. Coconut sugar can be used directly to replace regular sugar. This healthy sweetener has a delightful caramel taste.

Maple Syrup
This is an excellent alternative sweetener, boasting loads of antioxidants.

Brown Rice Syrup
Made from soaked and sprouted rice and cooked with an enzyme to break it down and turn into a sweet syrup. Rice syrup is fructose free and offers a great thick syrup sweetener.

Spices & Herbs

An essential addition to the Kind Earth pantry, for vibrancy, aliveness and divine culinary alchemy. You can buy dried herbs and spices to keep in store. They are often available in whole or ground form. Some spices are also readily available fresh and are excellent to have if you use them frequently. Grow your own herbs and enjoy that aliveness.

Keep herbs and spices that you know feature regularly in the recipes that you make...

Dried Spices & Herb Suggestions
- Turmeric • Cinnamon • Ground coriander • Cumin • Parsley • Curry blend • Ginger
- Cardamom pods • Fennel seeds • Black pepper • Onion powder • Nutmeg (whole)

Fresh Herbs & Spices
Grow in pots on the windowsill or in the garden: basil, coriander, parsley, rosemary, mint. Fresh to keep in the fridge or cool place: ginger, garlic, turmeric

Helpful Gluten-free Flours

√ *Great for conscious kitchen baking*
√ *Good shelf life*

Keeping your favourite gluten-free flours in stock is really helpful when you suddenly feel the urge to bake. I tend to use the same flours for different recipes. Unlike wheat flour, gluten-free baking often requires more than one flour to work synergistically to create wonderful baked goods. There are lots of options out there but I mostly use rice flour, tapioca flour and oat flour (or ground oats).

Brown Rice Flour
Rice flour is made from finely milled rice and is often the main flour used in my baked goods. It can also be used as a thickening agent. You can usually buy white or brown rice flour, but if at all possible go for the brown rice version for the higher nutritional content. Brown rice flour can be slightly gritty at times in baking, although it seems to work really well in combination with other flours.

Tapioca Flour
This is one ingredient in my kitchen that isn't particularly high in nutrients. Its purpose is much more functional, acting in combination with rice flour to produce delicious melt-in-the-mouth baked goods. It comes from the cassava plant and is sometimes called tapioca starch. You can also buy 'cassava flour' and use it as a direct replacement for tapioca flour. The difference between the two is that tapioca flour is a starch extracted from the cassava root through a process of washing and pulping. The wet pulp is squeezed to extract a starchy liquid. Once all the water evaporates from the starchy liquid, the tapioca flour remains; whereas, cassava flour is the whole root, simply peeled, dried and ground. Tapioca flour is also a great thickening agent for sauces.

Chickpea Flour (also known as gram flour)
This is an excellent flour made from chickpeas. You can use without other flours to create baked pakoras (see page 92) or crustless quiche (see page 124). It has a distinctive flavour, working best along with flavoursome herbs and spices. Chickpea flour is excellent for absorbing liquids. It's traditionally used in Indian dishes as a batter for bhajis and pakoras as well as Italian farinata or socca (which are a sort of cross between a pancake and bread).

Oat Flour
You can make quickly and easily by grinding down rolled oats. It's handy for baking with and in energy balls.

Superfoods

Here are some essential superfoods. Add any favourites that you discover along the way.

Cacao Powder
Essential ingredient for making healthy chocolate. Loaded with feel-good benefits. Always buy fairly traded, organic cacao products.

Cacao Butter
Important ingredient for homemade chocolate.

Lucuma Powder
A natural sweetener and nutritious dried fruit from South America. An excellent addition to superfood chocolate. Gives an other-worldly caramel taste to superfood sweet treats and sauces.

Super Green Powder
This is great if you want to make superfood smoothies. Try barley grass powder, wheatgrass powder, spirulina or moringa. They all have exceedingly awesome concentrated doses of minerals, vitamins, antioxidants and phyto-nutrients.

Matcha Powder
Exceptionally high in antioxidants, matcha powder is made consciously from green tea leaves in a way that preserves their natural integrity. The best comes from Japan - always buy organic.

Condiments & Helpful Extras

Here is a very simple list of those little things that can make a big difference to our cuisine.

Sea Salt
A good quality, unrefined sea salt is more nutritious than table salt. Table salt, on the other hand, has been stripped of its nutrients and has anti-caking agents added to it.

Passata
Passata is sieved tomatoes with a smooth, sauce like consistency. An excellent base ingredient.

Tamari or Shoyu
Tamari and shoyu are both fermented forms of soya sauce, ideal for sprinkling and last minute flavouring on rice, grains or salads. Tamari is usually gluten-free, whereas sometimes shoyu is made with a small amount of wheat.

Apple Cider Vinegar
A great addition to salad dressings, apple cider vinegar is also nice to add to tomato sauces and stir-fries. It is essential for Kind Earth kitchen baked cakes that require rising from the alchemical action of bicarbonate of soda.

Vanilla Extract
Essential ingredient for sweet treats. Life just wouldn't be the same without vanilla.

Healthy Fats & Oils

√ Excellent source of essential fats
√ Great for sauces and dressings

Almond Butter
Highly nutritious and excellent for spreading on rice cakes for a quick snack when the mood strikes.

Tahini
Tahini is made from ground sesame seeds. Be sure to buy a brand that makes a creamy tahini, as brands vary in taste and texture. Dark tahini is made from unshelled sesame seeds, whereas light tahini is made from hulled. Light usually has a more pleasant taste. Tahini is rich in phosphorus, magnesium and lecithin. It is also a great source of methionine, a liver detoxifier.

Creamed Coconut
Creamed Coconut (not to be confused with 'coconut cream') comes in a pure, solid, concentrated block that melts on heating. It is the unsweetened dehydrated fresh meat of a mature coconut, that has been ground in to a semi-solid white cream. It solidifies at normal room temperature. You can find it along with coconut milk in health food stores and it is often available in the world food section of a supermarket too. It is pretty much the same thing as coconut butter, although creamed coconut is usually less expensive to buy.

Oils
You can use oils as part of a healthy plant-based diet. Be sure to buy a good quality cold-pressed oil for raw use on salad dressings and coconut oil for sautéing and baking with.

Hemp Seed Oil
With its nutty flavour, this is an excellent choice for salad dressings. It has nature's perfect balance of omega 3 and omega 6 essential fatty acids.

Flaxseed Oil
Flaxseed, also known as linseed, is a great way to get omega 3 essential fats into your daily cuisine. It is high in ALA (alpha-linoleic acid). Flaxseed oil makes a great salad dressing ingredient although the taste is often an acquired one.

Coconut Oil
This oil is the best oil for cooking at high heat since it remains stable and doesn't breakdown to release free-radicals (unlike most other oils at high temperatures).

Whole grains

√ *Excellent shelf-life*
√ *Good for filling nutrient-rich meals*

Brown Rice
Brown rice still has its bran layer intact, which means that it retains significantly more nutrients than white rice. Excellent for B vitamins, manganese, selenium and phosphorus.

Quinoa
Quinoa is really a seed, used as a grain. It has an excellent nutritional profile and is a complete protein. Especially handy because it cooks in just 20 minutes. We can now buy local organic quinoa in Britain.

Millet
Millet offers excellent nutritional content. It is even faster to cook than quinoa. This grain has high levels of silica (which is good for skin, nails and hair). Millet also has an impressive array of minerals such as iron, phosphorous, magnesium, calcium and B vitamins.

Oats
Oats are full of protein and have a wonderful way of leaving you feeling full and nourished. They are good for B vitamins, phosphorous and iron. The manganese level in oats is very high - manganese helps to catalyse the bone building process in our body. Oats are also usually inexpensive.

Soba or Rice Noodles
These can be handy to have in… although obviously noodles aren't exactly a 'whole grain' because they've been turned into noodles. Soba is the Japanese name for buckwheat, which is a complete protein grain. Buy organic noodles, either buckwheat or rice, from a health food store. They cook in less than 5 minutes and are excellent to serve with a quick stir-fry or steamed veggies when you have little time to make dinner.

Grains that contain gluten
There are other grains such as spelt (the ancient cousin of wheat), barley and rye, which can be wonderful additions to your cuisine. They all contain gluten. I specialise in gluten-free cuisine which is why they don't appear in this book. However, if you are not gluten sensitive, then it should be fine to include them in your diet.

Pulses

√ *Excellent protein dense foods*
√ *Great shelf life*

What is a pulse? Is it a legume?
OK firstly there is the legume (any plant that grows in a pod). Pulse refers to the seed of a legume that has been DRIED. Beans, split peas, lentils and chickpeas are the most common types of pulses. Having been dried means that pulses have an excellent shelf life and can be safely stored. It's ideal to have some pulses in stock either in dried form or, if you want to be super-fast at times, have pre-cooked beans in cans or cartons.

TOP TIP:
Pulses can take a while to cook, so I like to cook a big batch in a pan all at once and then freeze them for later use.

Chickpeas
An essential pulse for hummus, salads, curry and bakes. Chickpeas have a slightly nutty-buttery flavour and hold their shape really well when frozen.

Lentils
You can get red, brown, green, black and dark speckled (also called puy or French green) lentils. Red is excellent for fast cooking and works well in soups, curries and dahl. Its shape disintegrates pretty quickly. The other types hold their shape incredibly well (especially puy lentils) and are good for cottage pies and bolognese dishes. I am usually sure to keep red and puy lentils in my kitchen at any one time.

Beans
There are lots of different types of beans that can be used for making bean burgers, bakes, adding to salads, soups and curries. They all have slightly different properties. Some keep their shape better than others, while some taste more nutty or are creamier. I always keep a couple of my favourites in stock such as black eyed beans and black beans.

www.ingramcontent.com/pod-product-compliance
Lightning Source LLC
Chambersburg PA
CBHW040507110526
44587CB00046B/4292